THE LEGACY LINK

THE LEGACY LINK

HOW TO BUILD A BULLETPROOF BUSINESS THAT OUTLASTS YOU

TESS HELMANDOLLAR

With thanks to Michelle O'Connor, of O'Connor Insurance Associates, for her insights for Chapter 20.

Statistics noted in Chapter One from JLL's 2025 U.S. Construction Outlook.

The Legacy Link: How to Build a Bulletproof Business That Outlasts You by Tess Helmandollar

First e-book edition, 2025

ISBN: 979-8-9988787-0-1 (e-book)

First print edition, 2025

ISBN: 979-8-9988787-1-8 (hardcover)

ISBN: 979-8-9988787-2-5 (paperback)

Design & Pagination: The Cognitive Creative, LLC

For My Daddy

CONTENTS

FOREWORD

The American Dream, we all want a piece of it. We are promised that if we work hard, focus forward, and give it our all, we will inevitably succeed and earn that piece of the pie we knew somewhere deep down was always ours. And that may be true, but what happens once we've succeeded? What happens once we've established the dream? If it's *our* dream, if it resides *solely* in our hearts and minds, what happens when we have to step away? Does the dream die?

If you have never learned the 10 pillars of Transferable Value, then it's highly likely that will be the case. It's a shame, but you have the tool in your hand to prevent just this fate.

In *The Legacy Link*, master wordsmith Tess Helmandollar takes us through the devastating loss of her dad, Link's, business, one that could not be saved no matter how they tried to resurrect the robust and successful operation he had once created. Why? Because the business resided in his heart, and almost entirely in his head. He had no systems, no predictable income stream, no employees, and no way to move forward...without him.

With humor and pith injected at every turn, Tess masterfully outlines the steps one must take to ensure that their business is, indeed, bulletproof. With real-life anecdotes and plenty of examples of people and businesses Tess has worked with personally, the book weaves best practices into the stories that leave an impression well after the pages have turned.

When it comes to your business, whether you step away intentionally, find someone else to run it, or want to sell, many lack the acumen to preplan effectively, which hinders their ability to set themselves up for long-term success. This book is the antidote to the certain death of your dream.

As I read through the pages, it hit me: I didn't have these pillars in place in *my own* business. Not even close. The realization was sobering. But Tess doesn't leave you in fear—she walks you forward, point by point, from "I have no idea where to start" to "I know exactly what to do next."

Few books like this exist that so clearly outline actionable steps to help one build a better and stronger business. And the steps are not mountains to climb; they are achievable, attainable goals you can set for yourself one right after the other. What's left in your wake will certainly be a business, a dream, that is built to survive even once it's time for the dreamer to pass the torch.

With its easy formatting and quick tempo, this book makes for exceptional reading material or a valuable reference tool while on the job. It even goes beyond basic business strategies to focus on how to be the kind of leader everyone with a team wants to be, helping you understand how to build and maintain a business with a winning culture, perhaps one of the most important aspects of any successful enterprise.

Don't wait until your health is failing. Don't wait until a crisis arises. Get this book and read it. Then, take the steps that are outlined in the text to ensure that your dream—your hard work, blood, sweat, and tears—will outlast you in even the most treacherous of circumstances.

❄

This book didn't just shape my thinking. It saved my business. Before *The Legacy Link*, I had what I called a "job." Now I'm building something that will outlast me—something that has the chance to become a true legacy. The kind of legacy Link Helmandollar would be proud of.

Lacey Knight,

Author, Founder, and CEO of Envisioned Equestrian

INTRODUCTION:
WHEN HARD WORK ISN'T ENOUGH

The crawl space was dark, the kind of darkness that swallowed everything except the weak glow of a flashlight. I followed my father on my hands and knees, and sometimes belly-crawling through cobwebs and chunks of Georgia red clay, the scent of damp earth thick in the air. He moved forward without hesitation, his Dickies work pants streaked with dirt, his typical gray t-shirt clinging to his back with sweat. He always had a pocket on his shirt, filled with pens, small tools, and a little bitty notebook, usually from Johnstone Supply. As we inched closer to the HVAC unit, those items tumbled out. I collected them, shoving them into the back pocket of my jeans.

At that moment, I wasn't thinking about the awkwardness of the ductwork we were dragging behind us or the oppressive Southern heat that would engulf us when we finally emerged from the crawl space. I was watching him. He was fearless in tackling the hardest problems, whether that meant digging an eighteen-foot trench by hand with a mattock and shovel, crawling into the dark with a flashlight between his teeth, or climbing an extension ladder with tools in one hand and equipment in the other. My father didn't just work hard; he worked with purpose. He solved problems that no one else wanted to deal with. No matter the environment, you could count on Dad to show up with a work ethic, tools, and solutions.

It never occurred to me back then that one day, those calloused hands and that relentless determination wouldn't be enough.

My father, William Lincoln Helmandollar, known as Link, wasn't just another small business owner; He was the embodiment of resilience. He was the kind of craftsman who could resurrect anything: old schoolhouses, failing HVAC systems, broken-down appliances, and who built his own livelihood from the ground up. But his greatest lesson didn't come from the homes he repaired or the systems he restored. It came from the business we couldn't save.

Deep in the Appalachians, in the coal belt of southern West Virginia, Dad was born into a world where hard work wasn't just expected, it meant basic survival. Asco, West Virginia, was one of many coal camps where families depended on each other for food and other goods that we take for granted today. He, his mom, and siblings often relied on extended family just to get by. That experience, I believe, shaped him more than he ever admitted. It made him determined. It made him skilled. And it left him with an underlying fear (one he never fully escaped) of ending up back in that place of scarcity.

So, he worked. Hard. With faith and skill, he built a life far removed from the one he grew up in. But that deep-rooted fear of not having enough never fully left him. I think that's why he held onto his business so tightly, even when he should have been building an exit plan.

After serving as an Aircraft Electrician in the U.S. Navy from 1970 to 1977, Dad settled in Georgia, where he worked as a Quality Assurance Engineer for a satellite manufacturing facility. When he was laid off in 1985, he didn't waste time licking his wounds. Instead, he turned to the work he knew best: fixing things. Link's Home Repair was born.

What started as side projects for friends and neighbors quickly grew into a full-fledged business. Over the next three decades, Dad built a company with over three hundred loyal customers and an annual revenue between $500,000 and $750,000. Often, he ran the business alone, not because he had to, but because he was the kind of man who believed he should. He was grateful, and sometimes that gratitude caused a misalignment with growth. My dad felt indebted to his clients for the prosperity his work granted him.

His customers weren't just clients; they were people he took care of. He watched families evolve, fixed broken toys for the kids, and made himself indispensable to them. He worked nights, weekends, whenever someone needed him. And they loved him for it.

Then, on June 28, 2018, a day after his sixty-eighth birthday, everything changed. A brain stem stroke. The kind that should have killed him.

At first, we thought he had beaten the odds. He was alive. His mobility was largely intact. And, for a little while, he still seemed like himself. Six weeks after the stroke, he even installed a new HVAC system. However, it was harder than it should have been, and he needed assistance in a way he never had before.

His reflexes were slower. His balance was off. His memory also seemed to be slightly affected. Because Dad was able to walk, talk, and even advocate for himself, his neurologist felt that perhaps the stroke, his high blood pressure, and his mild cognitive issues were caused by sleep apnea. In the midst of trying to figure all of this out, another blow came: a tumor in his lower jaw. Though not cancerous, the tumor forced the removal and reconstruction of his lower jaw and teeth. He endured this grueling surgery —and a subsequent one— like a champ.

If Dad's core memories were fading, we weren't aware. He

would just forget what he was talking about. We thought that was related to the stroke, and we were told that a CPAP machine would improve his cognitive issues. (It didn't.)

Then the COVID-19 pandemic hit, and we couldn't even *reach* the neurologist, let alone see him. I was terrified to take my parents out in public, especially Dad, after the ordeal he'd suffered. So, we waited. Dad started losing weight. We blamed that on his inability to eat as he once did. He knew us, but he stopped talking to us as much. When he did try to have a conversation, he got frustrated easily, telling us that he couldn't keep his thoughts straight.

A slow, creeping realization sank in that we were dealing with something new. We would later learn that the symptoms we had blamed on the stroke were actually Alzheimer's. Likely early-onset, made worse by the trauma of the stroke, and possibly his mandible resection and reconstruction, too.

Dad wanted to keep working. He talked about it. But the business, his multiple six-figure income, the company he built from nothing, had disintegrated when he could no longer show up for it. There was no transferable value. Link's Home Repair didn't die because Dad wasn't successful, or because he hadn't built something remarkable. It died because he hadn't built it to outlive him.

I fought for that business. I tried to piece together thirty-three years of knowledge, invoices, customer records, everything that had existed mostly in his head. But it wasn't enough. The systems weren't there. The right documentation wasn't there. The pieces of transferable value, contracts, automation, and strategic planning weren't there.

So, we lost it.

I've spent years since then helping business owners avoid that fate because my father's story and the story of Link's Home Repair aren't unique. Across service-based industries, business owners spend their lives working *in* their business, not *on* it. They believe they have time to figure out succession planning, documentation, or selling the company.

Yet, they don't.

None of us knows what's around the corner. And when the moment comes, it's too late. I would sit across from any service-based business owner today and tell them:

- The time to start building transferable value was *yesterday*.
- Stop thinking you'll always be the one doing the work. *You won't*.
- Stop believing that your customers will wait for you. *They won't*.
- Stop assuming your business will be worth something if you don't plan for it. *It won't*.

Get your ego out of the way. Sure, you can do all the things. But you *shouldn't*.

Delegation isn't weakness; it's survival.

I wish I had known then what I know now.

If Dad had been given just five more years of good health, we could have locked in maintenance contracts for at least 100–150 of his clients. That alone could have sustained my mother for years. Or maybe, if the stroke had never happened at all, he'd still be working today. He might have never retired, but at least he would have had the choice. Instead, the business he built with his own two hands died on the vine, and then he withered right behind it.

And yet, the legacy remains.

To this day, my father's old phone still rings. Years later, clients are still seeking his help. His name still carries weight in the community. People tell me all the time, *"I sure wish I could call your dad."*

But I don't just think about the business he left behind. I think about the life he didn't get to fully live because of how everything changed after the stroke. Retirement should have been about rest and reward, after decades of hard work. Instead, it was filled with:

- Doctors' visits
- Home health aides
- Frustration at the things he could no longer do

We took one big trip, to the Grand Canyon, a place my dad should have been able to stand in awe of. A place he should have soaked in with wonder. And yet, most of the time... he didn't really know where we were.

He got to fly a few times with my oldest son, Wade, sitting in the co-pilot seat, moments that should have made him brim with questions and beam with pride.

But he didn't have the cognitive clarity to fully experience it the way he would have just five years earlier.

And my youngest son, Wyatt, the baby of our family?

For the last 6 months of his life, Dad rarely knew him.

That's what was stolen from him. Not just the business. The time.

Lost time: it's what so many business owners never see coming.

We think we have decades to figure things out.

We think we'll know when it's time to step back.

We think we'll get the retirement we deserve.

But life doesn't always give us that choice.

This book exists so that one day, no one will have to say that about you.

Your business, your life's work, shouldn't disappear when you do.

It should live on. Supporting:

Your family

Your employees

Your legacy

The next chapters will show you exactly how to make that happen.

But first, be brutally honest with yourself:

Are you building something that can outlive you?

Or are you just running out the clock?

CHAPTER 1
THE CURRENT LANDSCAPE

NAVIGATING CHALLENGES AND OPPORTUNITIES IN THE CONSTRUCTION AND SERVICE INDUSTRIES

Let's be real: most businesses don't start with a spreadsheet or a five-year plan. They start with a skill, a little courage, and a maxed-out credit card.

You don't need an MBA to know how to fix what's broken, build something that lasts, or take care of people. That's how my dad, Link, built his HVAC business. That's how a lot of good businesses get built... with grit, not guidance.

But here's the catch: what gets you started won't always keep you going. And it definitely won't keep your business alive if something happens to you.

My dad had a great reputation, loyal customers, steady income, but when life threw him a curveball, everything he'd built was suddenly at risk. Not because it wasn't real, but because it wasn't ready to outlast him.

Most small businesses don't build exit strategies; they're too busy making payroll and keeping the lights on. Even the ones that grow, hire a team, and pull in serious revenue often miss the deeper foundation that makes a business *transferable*.

A business can look like a success with steady cash flow, a good reputation, and work on the books for months. It can serve the community, create jobs, and feel like a real win. But sometimes? That success is a house of cards. Built on hustle, not systems. On the owner's back, not a structure that could stand without them.

My dad's story is a powerful example of that truth. By every traditional measure, his business was solid: loyal customers, a steady income, decades of earned trust. But when life hit hard, none of that was enough to keep it going.

He didn't fail. But the business couldn't function without him, and that's a reality many owners don't face until it's too late.

Today's construction and service industries aren't slowing down to give anyone time to figure it out. The ground is shifting, faster than most of us would like.

Economic swings, tech changes, labor shortages, new customer demands... these aren't hypotheticals. They're the current playing field. And if you're still running on instinct alone, you're at risk.

In this chapter, we'll dig into what's really happening out there, the trends, the pressure points, and the opportunities. Whether you're a solo operator like Link or running a full team, you need to know what's changing so you can stop reacting and start preparing.

Because behind every market stat and every shift in the field? There's a business owner trying to build something that lasts. That's who this book is for. That's who I'm writing to.

FROM ONE BUSINESS TO AN ENTIRE INDUSTRY

My dad's story isn't just his; it's the story of thousands of business owners across the trades. The kind of people who built something out of nothing. They've got the skills, the reputation, and the work ethic... but not always the roadmap for what comes next.

Here's the hard truth: the world isn't waiting for them to figure it out.

The construction and service industries are shifting under our feet. The challenges are real, but so are the opportunities, if you know where to look.

So, let's talk about what's coming and how to make sure your business isn't just surviving. Let's set it up to WIN!

INDUSTRY-WIDE CHALLENGES AND TRENDS (A.K.A. WHAT'S COMING FOR YOUR BUSINESS AND HOW TO STAY AHEAD OF IT)

The construction and service industries right now? Think Monday morning on a job site: chaotic, unpredictable, and just a little too loud.

Some surprises are good, like landing a dream client who actually pays on time. Others make you question every life choice you've ever made.

Like it or not, the game is changing. Fast.

Let's walk through what's shifting and how you can protect your business from getting blindsided by the economy, labor shortages, tech changes, or whatever else the future decides to throw your way.

1. The Economy: A Rollercoaster Without a Seatbelt

According to JLL's 2025 U.S. Construction Outlook, the industry is expected to see modest growth after a stretch of whiplash years, from booming, to brutal, to "Meh, could be worse."

Translation? There's money to be made. But it's not falling from the sky.

The companies that win will be the ones that:

- Plan ahead
- Streamline their operations
- And don't get caught flat-footed when the next curveball comes

2. The Labor Shortage: Where Did Everybody Go?

You've seen it firsthand: good help is hard to find. And when you finally do land someone solid, another company tries to poach them before their boots are even broken in.

The next generation? Not exactly lining up for trade school. Somewhere along the way, they all got convinced that massive student debt and sitting in meetings about meetings was better than wiring a building or laying perfect tile.

That's left us with a massive gap.

The fix? Culture.

If you're running a company like a narcissistic parent, where "benefits" mean working 'only' a half-day on holidays, Christmas bonuses come in the form of expired coupons, and responsibility is handed out without a shred of authority, you'll end up a solid team of one. Especially if you're walking around with a magnifying glass like it's part of your uniform.

But what if you built something people actually want to be part of? A place with fair pay, real training, PTO that doesn't come with retribution, and actual respect for your crew?

You'd stand out for all the right reasons. And you'd keep the good ones from walking out the door.

3. Costs Are Rising (Shocking, Right?)

After a weird little breather in 2024, construction costs are climbing again, possibly around 5% to 7% in 2025 (maybe more), depending on how the tariff roulette wheel lands.

Translation? Everything's getting more expensive: materials, labor, insurance, fuel, all of it.

So what do you do?

- Plan ahead: No more last-minute material runs that kill your margins and your mood.
- Use tech to stay organized: Even basic tools for invoicing and scheduling can save you thousands.

- Raise your prices: If your rates haven't changed since your logo was designed in Microsoft Paint, you're already under water.

4. Supply Chains: Like Smokey and the Bandit, But for Plywood

There was a stretch when getting your hands on lumber felt like running backroads with a load of bootleg 2x4s, except instead of outrunning the law, you were chasing down suppliers who "thought they had it in stock."

And even now? It's still rough. Prices are unpredictable. Lead times shift by the hour. And sometimes, the supplier just flat-out lies to you. You drive out expecting three dozen 2x2s for porch railing, and it turns out ol' Cletus counted lattice strips instead.

That ain't holding back a two-year-old on a sugar rush, much less meeting code.

So, how do you deal with it?

- Order early — way earlier than you think you need to.
- Have backups — and then backups for your backups.
- Communicate clearly — so clients don't blame you for delays you couldn't control if you had a forklift and a magic wand.

5. Technology: The Post-It Note Stuck To Your Rear Is...Ineffective.

Sure, the laser level had its moment, but let's not pretend the construction industry is known for embracing cutting-edge tech. Most businesses still run on gut instinct, whiteboards, and whatever fell out of the glovebox.

That sticky note? You sat on it. (See above.)

But here's the thing: the companies that *do* use technology? They're pulling ahead. Fast.

Here's what's actually making a difference:

- AI-powered scheduling and cost estimation: Because "I think it'll take about two days" is how jobs turn into money pits. Good tech can give you better predictions *and* tighter margins.
- GPS tracking for equipment: No more "Where the hell is the Bobcat?" moments. (It's in the wrong county. Again.)
- Digital project management: Paperwork doesn't just slow you down; it costs you. Systems that track jobs, timelines, and changes in one place keep profit from leaking out the side.
- Integrated tools that talk to each other: If your scheduling app, CRM (customer relationship management), and invoicing software can't communicate, you're wasting time. Tech should reduce chaos, not add to it.
- 3D modeling and visual quoting tools: Clients love seeing what they're paying for. And when you can walk them through the job before a hammer ever swings? You look like the pro you are.

And if all that sounds like overkill, don't worry, you don't need a NASA control center. You just need a system that works for *your* business. (We'll talk more about that later.)

6. Green Building: Not Just for Hippies Anymore

Like it or not, sustainability isn't a fringe concept anymore. Whether or not the feds are enforcing it, clients are still asking for it. Local codes are still tightening. And energy efficiency? That's just smart business.

You don't need to build solar-powered treehouses, but you *do* need to understand how high-efficiency systems, sustainable materials, and eco-friendly design can become a major competitive advantage.

The bonus? You can often charge premium prices, reduce call-backs, and position yourself as the forward-thinking option without reinventing your entire business.

7. The Housing Market: The Wild, Wild West

Corporate investors like BlackRock are snatching up single-family homes faster than first-time buyers can get financing. Meanwhile, new housing policies will shake things up over the next few years.

For builders and contractors, this means opportunities, but only if you're paying attention to where demand is shifting. Whether it's home renovations, multi-family construction, or adaptive reuse projects (turning old buildings into new housing), staying flexible is the name of the game, especially when it feels like the rules change every time you pour a slab.

8. The Cost of Money

In construction, understanding the cost of money, meaning the interest rates tied to borrowing, is crucial. For years, low rates helped fuel growth in both residential and commercial projects. But now? Things are tightening up.

Thanks to recent shifts in monetary policy, borrowing has gotten a lot more expensive. Land acquisition, lot development, construction loans, it's all getting pricier. And that's before you even see a blueprint.

HISTORICAL RESILIENCE AMID ECONOMIC CHALLENGES

This isn't the first time the industry's taken a hit from rising interest rates. Back in the early '80s, we saw double-digit rates while the Fed tried to wrangle inflation with both hands. And yet, construction adapted, leaning into renovations and energy efficiency instead of betting the farm on brand-new builds.

TODAY'S LANDSCAPE

We're seeing the same pattern now. With the Fed tightening policy, builders are scaling back in certain sectors, especially residential, where higher mortgage rates are making buyers flinch.

Bottom line?

Your projects need to pencil out. That means smarter forecasting, tighter margins, and a little creativity, because just "waiting it out" won't keep the lights on.

STRATEGIES FOR NAVIGATING HIGHER BORROWING COSTS

In light of these challenges, construction professionals can consider several strategies:

1. Diversify, but do it strategically

Yes, remodeling and commercial work are less rate-sensitive than new builds, but diversification doesn't just mean "do more kinds of jobs." It means identifying *where your existing team and equipment* can serve a parallel market with less overhead or faster turnaround. Think:

- Pivoting to service contracts or specialty installations
- Focusing on retrofits for energy efficiency (especially with upcoming incentives)
- Partnering with GC firms for commercial TI work if you're usually residential

Don't chase every shiny opportunity. Expand *intelligently,* where you already have traction or can scale quickly.

2. Stop the leaks before you chase more water. (*A.K.A. Operational Efficiency, but real*)

Rising interest rates aren't just about borrowing; they expose every inefficiency in your business. If you're:

- Replacing lost invoices weekly
- Rebuying tools you "definitely had"
- Paying overtime because of scheduling gaps

...you're not ready to take on higher-cost capital.
This is the moment to lean into system audits:

- What workflows waste time?
- What gets done twice because nobody's talking?
- Where are you bleeding profit, and not just spending it?

This is where tech earns its keep, and good systems can help lock it down.

3. Strengthen your cash position *and* your leverage.

Healthy reserves are great, but even if you don't have a six-figure cushion, you can improve your financing leverage by:

- Cleaning up your books (lender's notice)
- Reducing aged receivables
- Negotiating vendor terms now, *before* you're in a pinch
- Building strong banking relationships while you're still stable

And if you're considering equipment financing or a line of credit? Don't wait until rates go even higher. Move now, while your credit picture is stronger than your next three months might be.

4. Looking Ahead

Higher borrowing costs bring undeniable challenges, but they also force innovation. The businesses that adapt, get lean, and think strategically are the ones that will stay standing.

Understand the pressure points. Strengthen your systems. Plan smarter.

You don't have to overhaul everything overnight, but you *do* have to start thinking like a business owner, not just a tradesperson.

BOTTOM LINE: YOU CAN'T AFFORD TO WING IT ANYMORE

The construction and service industries are shifting fast. The companies that plan ahead and build real systems will thrive. The ones that don't? They'll spend the next few years stuck in survival mode.

But here's the good news:

- You don't have to do everything at once.
- You don't need to be a tech genius or an economist.
- You just need to build a business that works for *you*, not the other way around.

That's what this book is here to help you do.

Not just a paycheck.

Not just a job.

A business with backbone, vision, and value.

A business that lasts.

CHAPTER 2
LEGACY ON PURPOSE

DON'T YOU DARE WASH THE CAST IRON, OR BUILD A BUSINESS THAT CAN'T BE PASSED DOWN

(WHY I CARE *THIS* MUCH)

Before we get too deep into strategies and structures, I want to slow down for just a moment and offer a hand on your shoulder.

You've already done a lot of emotional lifting by reading this far. You've looked at the truth of your industry, maybe even the truth of your own business, and now we're heading into the part of the book where we build: the frameworks, models, and checklists that can change everything.

But before we go there, I need you to know why this matters to me, why I didn't just write a manual, and why I filled these pages with stories that carry humor, heart, and real life...because otherwise, this stuff can feel dry, even though it's the lifeblood of legacy.

My story doesn't begin with a business plan. It begins in the Appalachian mountains, at the kitchen tables and church pews of women who raised me to show up fully and speak the truth.

My Aunt Peggy taught me that being true to myself might disappoint people I love, and that's okay. She saw me clearly in my most vulnerable moments and reminded me I didn't have to be perfect to be powerful.

My Sissy, my Aunt Loretta, was my summertime bridge to a family eight hours away. I spent childhood summers in West Virginia with her and my cousins, who became my surrogate siblings. I learned about relationships, laughter, and chaos in the most beautiful way; lessons I would have missed as an only child. Lessons I would need for raising three of my own.

And when I stood beside Sissy in churches, singing at revivals and high-attendance services, I found my voice, literally and figuratively. That's where my confidence began: five years old, banging a tambourine and singing half-memorized lyrics next to someone who believed in me.

And then there's my mother, the one who raised me with unwavering love and a perfect dose of humility.

She often told me during my teenage years, "You're not conceited, you're just convinced." That playful nudge gave me the permission I needed to take messy action, to start businesses, to tell stories, and to write this book. Without her steady support and truth-telling, none of this would exist.

So if anything in these pages has felt like it came from somewhere deeper than marketing strategy or operational advice... it did.

It came from them.

From a grandmother who was a minister's wife, a butcher with an eighth-grade education, and a genius for math.

From a father who built with his hands and loved with his presence.

From a family who believed in doing things well, doing them fully, and sometimes, yes, doing them with the wrong sugar. Because doing it with love often requires creativity, beyond what the spec can show.

I'll tell you that story one day.

This is where my voice comes from.

I also have my grandmother Sylvia's cast-iron skillets. One of them, I believe, was her mother Rosa's. Everyone said Rosa was mean, but I didn't know her. What I do know is this: I've carried that skillet across state lines and multiple kitchens. It's made a million cakes of cornbread, the occasional pot pie, and enough peach cobbler to put all of Towns County into a sugar coma.

I can cook over a fire with it or bake in a modern oven. In a pinch, I could use it as a weapon, and in some ways, maybe I have.

You care for a skillet like that. You season it, protect it, and hand it down. It's simple, utilitarian, a survival tool that becomes a legacy.

So let me ask you this: if we treat a piece of cookware with that kind of reverence, why don't we treat our businesses the same way?

It's time to change that.

Let's build something that lasts.

THRIVING IN A SHIFTING INDUSTRY

The construction and service sectors are evolving fast, and businesses, whether in residential, commercial, industrial, or specialty trades, can't afford to sit back and hope for the best. Long-term success isn't about working harder; it's about working smarter. The key? Mastering the Ten Pillars that create true transferable value, so your business isn't just surviving, but thriving, even without you at the helm. Here's where to focus:

THE TEN PILLARS OF A BUSINESS THAT OUTLIVES YOU

1. Know Where You're Going (Strategic Planning) – If you don't have a map, you're just wandering. Set a

clear vision, define where you want to be in 5, 10, or 15 years, and start making moves *now* to get there.

2. Keep More of Your Money (Financial Management) – A thriving business doesn't just make money, it *keeps* it. Cash flow, budgeting, pricing, and smart investments aren't optional; they're survival tools.

3. Work Smarter, Not Harder (Operational Efficiency) – If everything falls apart when you step away, you don't have a business; you have a very stressful job. Automate, delegate, and build systems that *don't* need you 24/7.

4. Use Tech Before It Uses You (Technology Integration) – AI, CRM, Cyber Security, Secure Networks, and automation, these aren't just buzzwords; they're tools that make your life easier. Learn what's out there and *actually use it* before your competitors do. You may find that you're behind the eight ball.

5. Be Seen, Be Remembered (Marketing & Branding) – If no one knows who you are, it doesn't matter how great your work is. Build a brand and a reputation that attracts customers on autopilot.

6. Build a Crew That Stays (Workforce Development) – Hiring is hard. Keeping good people is harder. Create a culture, offer real benefits, and make your company a place where people *want* to work.

7. Keep Customers Coming Back (Customer Relationship Management) – One-and-done jobs won't cut it. Build service contracts, loyalty programs, and a customer experience that keeps them choosing *you*.

8. Don't Put All Your Eggs in One Basket (Diversification & Market Expansion) – Relying on one revenue stream is a risk you can't afford. Expand

your services, tap into new markets, and stay ahead of industry shifts.

9. Don't Get Fined or Shut Down (Sustainability & Compliance) – Keeping up with regulations, safety standards, and green building practices isn't just a good idea, it's how you avoid lawsuits and fines.

10. Plan Your Exit (Exit Strategy & Succession Planning) – You *will* leave your business one day, by choice or by force. Make sure it's on *your* terms, with a plan that gets you paid and keeps your company alive.

Let's be real, most business owners don't wake up thinking about *transferable value*. They're thinking about making payroll, dealing with a customer who suddenly "doesn't remember" agreeing to that change order, or figuring out how to keep their best employee from jumping ship to a competitor.

But here's the thing: this stuff *matters*. Not just for some far-off day when you decide to retire or sell (although, spoiler alert: that day comes faster than you think). It matters *right now*.

Change is the only constant in the construction and service industries. Costs are rising. Skilled labor is getting harder to find. Customers expect more for less. And technology is changing the way we do business, whether we like it or not. You can either *own* those changes or get steamrolled by them.

Building a business with real, transferable value doesn't just mean you'll have something to sell one day; it means your company *runs better today*. It means you have fewer fires to put out because you've built systems that work. It means you can take a vacation (a *real* one, not just checking emails from the beach). It means your team actually sticks around because they see a future in working for you.

So, yeah, this stuff isn't just about an exit plan. It's about making sure your business isn't running *you* into the ground. And if you do it right, one day, when you *do* decide to step away, you won't have to walk away empty-handed.

The next chapter is where we get into the nuts and bolts of *how* you make that happen. No fluff, no theory, just real strategies to help you build a business that lasts. Let's get to it.

WHY SHOULD YOU CARE? (NO, REALLY.)

Alright, let's be honest. You didn't pick up this book because you were dying to read industry reports or get a crash course in economic policy. You picked it up because, at some point, you realized that just being damn good at what you do isn't enough.

You're out there every day, working harder than half the population even knows how to. You're the one crawling under houses, climbing onto roofs, wiring up entire buildings, and solving problems that people don't even realize exist.

And yet, when it comes to the actual business side of things? That's where things get...messy.

Maybe you've had that heart-drop moment where you realize your business depends entirely on you. Maybe you've wondered what happens when you can't be on the job site every day. Or maybe you've watched another contractor or service business crash and burn when the owner stepped away, and you thought, "Damn, that could be me."

Here's the thing: it doesn't have to be.

This book isn't here to tell you to work harder. You already do that. It's here to help you work smarter. To make sure that everything you've built, the blood, sweat, and caffeine-fueled late nights, actually means something when you're ready to step back.

Because here's the brutal truth:

- If your business dies the second you take a vacation, you don't own a business, you own a job.

- If no one but you knows how to keep things running, you're not running a company, you're holding it hostage.
- If your business isn't set up to survive without you, it's not worth nearly as much as you think it is.

And that's why this matters.

Not because I want you to spend your nights reading about financial statements and exit strategies (though, hey, maybe grab a sweet tea—or a beer—and skim those chapters when you get the chance). But because one day, whether it's by choice or by force, you're going to step away.

Will your business be worth something?

Or will it just disappear like you were never there?

That's what we're going to figure out together.

Now, buckle up. We've got work to do.

CHAPTER 3
UNDERSTANDING YOUR KPIS

KEY PERFORMANCE METRICS OR KILLER PLANS FOR INCOME!

Listen, I get it. The second someone starts talking about *business metrics*, your eyes glaze over like someone just handed you a 400-page instruction manual for a toaster. But hear me out, KPIs aren't just boring numbers on a spreadsheet. They're your business's way of telling you exactly how to make more money and avoid dumb mistakes. Remember: Killer Plans for Income.

Think of them like the gauges on a dashboard. If your truck's gas light comes on, you don't ignore it and hope for the best (well, most of us don't). KPIs do the same thing for your business. They tell you when you're running low, when something's off, and when it's time to step on the gas.

LINK'S BUSINESS, WHAT HE GOT RIGHT (AND WHERE KPIS COULD HAVE HELPED)

Let's talk about my dad, Link.

He wasn't flying blind; he used QuickBooks, and he knew when a job made him money or cost him money. He didn't need an MBA or some fancy dashboard to price his jobs correctly; he had a formula that worked, built on instinct, experience, and decades of knowing his trade inside and out.

But here's the catch: when you're slammed, tracking goes out the window.

Summertime in Georgia? It's hell's front porch. When the heat cranks up, AC units die faster than cheap flip-flops on hot pavement, and my dad? He ran 90 miles an hour from 7 AM to 8 PM nearly every single day. He wasn't sitting down analyzing spreadsheets. He was fixing, installing, and sweating through three shirts a day.

And that's where most business owners struggle.

When it's slow, you're watching every penny. But when you're buried in work? Tracking gets sloppy. Numbers get *fuzzy*. And that's when money starts leaking out of your business.

KPIS ARE JUST THE METRICS YOU ALREADY CARE ABOUT

Here's what I've learned after hundreds of conversations with business owners:

Everyone has a favorite metric.

They just don't realize it's a KPI.

It's hilarious when you get business owners talking about numbers, people get *fired up* about this like it's a BBQ debate. My friend and client, Travis at United Pump in Suwanee, GA, has so many flat tires he and his team have a "flat tire KPI". It's a joke ... of course, but see, a metric is a metric, be it serious, or fun and games.

Some guys track sales. If the numbers are up, everything must be great. (*Spoiler: Not always.*)

Some watch cash flow and ignore everything else. (*Until tax season punches them below the belt.*)

Some check the bank balance daily, if there's money in the

account, what's the problem? (*The problem is, that's a terrible way to run a business.*)

Some owners obsess over productivity, how many jobs got done that day. (*But if they're all underpriced? Not great.*)

And then there are the "gut feeling" guys. They track nothing, but "know" if business is good. (*No offense, if your gut is rumbling, it probably has more to do with the hot dog you ate for lunch than your finances.*)

The truth is, *all* of these numbers matter, but none of them alone give you the full picture.

KPIS? NEVER HEARD OF THEM. (AND THAT'S WHY YOU'RE LOSING MONEY)

Let's talk about what happens when you don't track your numbers. Because I promise you, whether you track them or not, they are happening anyway.

- If you don't track profit margins, you could be selling jobs at a loss. You're out there working 12-hour days, and for what? To break even?
- If you ignore customer acquisition costs, you might be paying $200 in ads to land a $150 job.
- If you don't monitor cash flow, you could be making plenty of money but still running out of cash before payroll hits.
- If you don't look at job profitability, you could be loading up on "busy work" that's actually dragging down your business.
- And if you don't track customer retention, you might be spending way too much time chasing new customers when you could be making more money from the ones you already have.

So, let me ask you, do you really know if every job is worth doing?

Or are you just *hoping* for the best?

THE DAY I HURT MY OWN FEELINGS OVER KPIS

Let's fast forward to me, sitting at my desk, thinking I have a solid handle on my business finances.

I track my income. I know my overhead. Hell, I have spreadsheets for days. I also have Nickie (my finance director), and thank the 8 lb 6 oz baby Jesus for her, or I would not have a dime to my name. I digress, one day, I decided to break down my actual costs per client.

So I made a tools-and-scope spreadsheet for my monthly clients. It showed everything included in my retainers, the tech stack, the management, the CRM, and the marketing tools.

And that's when I hurt my own feelings.

$6,500 a year in tools.

Included in ALL retainers, whether clients paid $1,000 a month or $5,000.

I was eating most of these costs. Sure, it's the cost of doing business, but my cost was too high. So I raised my prices. That day.

The kicker? I thought I had it all under control. I knew my numbers, or so I thought. But until I broke it down in black and white, I didn't see how much I was bleeding money.

That's what KPIs do. They show you what you don't want to see but need to know.

If you've ever wondered, '*Am I charging enough?*' or '*Why am I working this hard and still feel broke?*' This is why.

KPIS, EXPLAINED (FOR PEOPLE WHO'D RATHER BE DOING *LITERALLY* ANYTHING ELSE)

A *Key Performance Indicator* sounds like something a corporate consultant made up in a boardroom. But here's what it really is:

KPIs are the numbers that tell you whether your business is actually making money, where you're losing money, and what you need to fix before it's too late.

If you're thinking, *I don't have time to track all that*, let me ask you this:

- Do you know exactly how much it costs you to get a new customer?
- Do you know if you're actually making money on every job?
- Do you know which customers bring in the most profit vs. which ones are wasting your time?

If you answered *no* to any of these, congratulations! You are running your business in the dark.

Let's fix that.

THE 5 KPIS YOU ACTUALLY NEED TO TRACK OR HOW TO TELL IF YOU'RE WINNING (OR JUST WORKING OVERTIME)

Forget the 40-page spreadsheets and the MBA jargon. Here are five numbers that really matter if you want to know whether your business is working or slowly self-destructing in the background.

1. Revenue Growth Rate – Is Your Business Growing or Flatlining?

Formula:

(Current Revenue - Last Revenue) ÷ Last Revenue × 100

What it really means:

Are you making more money than you did last month or last year? If not, you're not growing, you're just getting busier for no reason.

2. Profit Margin – Are You Actually Keeping Any of This Money?

Formula:

Net Profit ÷ Revenue × 100

What it really means:

You made $10,000! Cool. But how much of that did you keep after bills, payroll, supplies, and that random $400 Home Depot run? If it's not much, you're working too hard for too little.

3. Customer Acquisition Cost (CAC) – Are You Bleeding Money to Get Clients?

Formula:

Total Marketing & Sales Costs ÷ Number of New Customers

What it really means:

If you spent $1,000 to get one $900 client, congrats! You paid $100 to work. That's an expensive and labor-intensive hobby. Not a business.

4. Customer Lifetime Value (CLV) – How Much Is Each Customer Really Worth?

Formula:

Average Sale × Times They Buy × How Long They Stick Around

What it really means:

If someone buys once and ghosts you, they're worth $200. If they come back five times a year for three years, they're worth thousands. Know who's who, and for the love of all that is holy, focus on the ones who stick.

5. Job Profitability – Are Some Jobs Secretly Costing You Money?

Formula:

(Revenue from Job - Total Job Cost) ÷ Revenue from Job

What it really means:

That big job that made you "look successful"? If it drained your crew, overran hours, and barely broke even, it's not a win, it's a lesson.

Bottom Line:

If you only track these five things, you'll catch 90% of what's hurting or helping your business. The rest can be helpful depending on your business, a lot are just noise (or fuel for your accountant's next vacation).

NOT A NUMBERS PERSON? HERE'S WHERE TO START WITHOUT DROWNING IN DATA

If KPIs sound like something your accountant made up to stress you out, you're not alone. But avoiding the numbers doesn't make the problem go away; it just makes it harder to spot when something's going sideways.

Here's how to get started, even if you've never cracked open QuickBooks:

1. Use Your Bank Account, But Don't Stop There

Your bank balance shows cash flow, but it doesn't show *profit*.

What to do: Once a week, write down your income and your expenses on a single sheet (or Google Sheet). Label it by week. You'll start to see patterns fast, like how your "good weeks" still bleed out from high expenses.

2. Track Jobs With a Simple Spreadsheet (That You Actually Use)

If you're brand new to this, you probably don't need software yet.

You need habits.

What to do: Create a one-line-per-job sheet with columns for:

- Job name

- Revenue
- Labor cost
- Materials cost
- Total expenses
- Profit

This gets you into the practice of tracking *real job profitability*, which will make you smarter with bids and help you avoid low-margin headaches.

3. Start a "Customer Value" List

You don't need to know every detail right now, but you need to know who's worth keeping.

What to do: List your last 10 customers.

Then write:

- What they paid
- How many times they bought
- Where they came from

This gets you used to thinking in terms of Customer Lifetime Value (CLV) and Customer Acquisition Cost (CAC), even if you're not using the full formulas yet.

4. Ask Your Bookkeeper (or Find One Who Speaks Human)

If you don't have a bookkeeper, get one, even part-time. Heck, even sometimes.

What to do: Ask them for these five numbers each month:

- Revenue
- Expenses
- Net profit
- CAC (or how much you spent on marketing vs. customers earned)
- Job profitability (even just a high-level view)

If they can't give you that clearly, it might be time for a new bookkeeper.

5. Pick One KPI and Track It for 30 Days

Start small. Don't worry about doing everything at once.

What to do: Choose one of the five KPIs (like profit margin) and write it down every week. Once you're used to seeing it, the next one will be easier.

Bottom line:

You don't need to turn into a CFO overnight, but you *do* need to stop flying blind. The more comfortable you get with the story your numbers are telling, the more power you'll have to steer your business in the right direction.

YOUR BUSINESS SHOULD TAKE CARE OF YOU, NOT THE OTHER WAY AROUND

Look, my dad worked himself to the bone because he believed in service, in helping people, in doing the job right. And I know that if he could do it over, he wouldn't have changed that.

But I *do* think he would have changed how he ran his business.

He would have built it so that it could take care of him in return.

He would have made sure it could run even if he had to step away.

Because at the end of the day, what's the point of working this hard if it all falls apart when you stop?

That's why this matters.

Not just for some *future you*, but for *right now*.

So, let's get serious about building a business that pays you back.

FINAL THOUGHT: KPIS = CASH IN YOUR POCKET

At the end of the day, KPIs aren't about data for the sake of data; they're about knowing exactly how to make your business more profitable, sustainable, and worth something when you're ready to step away.

So, yeah, this stuff is worth your time. And in the next chapter, we're going even deeper into how to make sure your business is actually keeping the money you work so damn hard for.

Let's get to it.

CHAPTER 4
FINANCIAL
FOUNDATIONS

UNDERSTANDING THE MONEY IN YOUR
BUSINESS (SO YOU'RE NOT ROBBING PETER TO
PAY PAUL)

It was February, and the work had slowed to a crawl, just like it did every single year.

My mom sat at the kitchen table with the checkbook in one hand and an unpaid equipment bill in the other.

The client's check was taking forever to clear because this was before electronic payments, before same-day transfers, before small businesses could count on instant cash flow.

She sighed, tapping into their savings to cover the bill. My dad, ever the optimist, gave her a reassuring smile and said:

"Sometimes we have to rob Peter to pay Paul." Without missing a beat, Mom shot back: "That works until Peter goes broke!"

And that was small business finances in a nutshell.

Money came in waves.

Expenses never stopped.

THE SMALL BUSINESS MONEY PROBLEM NO ONE TALKS ABOUT

The biggest financial mistake small business owners make?

Assuming more revenue = more profit.

It doesn't.

More revenue without a financial structure just makes you tired.

And this is where a lot of businesses struggle early on.

They work non-stop.

They have loyal customers.

They have skills no one else can match.

But if their financial system is built for survival, not success, it's a matter of time before the stress catches up.

HOW DAD MASTERED HIS BUSINESS FINANCES (THE RIGHT WAY, FAST)

When my dad started his business, I was 15 years old, which means I had no idea whether things were slow or not.

But I do know that he figured out the seasonal cycles of his business almost immediately.

After two seasons, he had it dialed in.

He and my mom started saving even more aggressively.

They adjusted for slow months before they happened.

They were already great savers, but the business meant they had to level up even further, and they did.

By the time the business was a decade old, they were able to take vacations in the slow months because they had built a financial buffer.

And here's another important point:

My dad NEVER borrowed money for the business.

He had excellent credit, but he never took out loans.

Everything was built debt-free.

That's rare. It also shows that he was risk-averse, and if he were here now, he would stand over me until I typed: NO RISK, NO REWARD!

It worked for him because he tracked his finances, knew what was coming, and adjusted quickly.

DO YOU EVEN KNOW WHERE YOUR MONEY GOES?

Let's talk about financial tracking, but don't worry, I promise not to make this feel like an accountant's PowerPoint presentation.

I once sat down with a business owner, and we had a conversation that went something like this:

Me: "How much do you make per job?"

Him: *"I don't know exactly, but it's pretty good."*

Me: "How much do you spend on materials?"

Him: *"I mean, I have a general idea."*

Me: "Okay... so what's your profit margin?"

Him: ... (*stares into the abyss like I just asked him to solve quantum physics in his head.*)

I know, I know. Nobody wakes up excited to analyze their profit margins over coffee. But here's the deal, if you don't know where your money is going, I promise you it's going somewhere you don't want it to.

And here's the biggest financial problem I see in service businesses: People think they have a revenue problem when they actually have a cash flow problem.

It's easy to assume that if you're not making the money you want, the solution is just "Get more jobs." But that's not always true. Sometimes, the real issue is that you're working harder than ever, but the money is leaking out faster than it's coming in. Maybe your pricing is off. Maybe your overhead is higher than you think. Maybe you're undercharging without even realizing it. Whatever the reason, if you don't track where every dollar is going, you'll keep running in circles, wondering why you're exhausted but your bank account looks like it's on a diet.

CASH FLOW IS KING (AND WHY BEING PROFITABLE DOESN'T MEAN YOU HAVE MONEY)

This is where business owners get tripped up all the time. You can look at your profit and loss statement and feel like a financial genius; your company is profitable, the numbers look great, and on paper, you're killing it. But then you check your bank account, and suddenly, reality hits. There's barely enough to cover payroll, and the vendor bill that's due next week? Let's just say you're not feeling as rich as those financial statements suggest.

The problem isn't that you're not making money. The problem is that cash flow and profit aren't the same thing.

Here's how it happens: A client owes you $10,000, but they haven't paid yet. Meanwhile, payroll is due, so you dip into savings, or worse, put materials on a credit card, because you have to keep things moving. In your head, you tell yourself, "It's fine. The money is coming." And it is... eventually. But now you're playing financial whack-a-mole, shifting money around, robbing Peter to pay Paul, and praying that Peter doesn't start charging interest.

It's an exhausting cycle, and the worst part? It can sneak up on you even when business is booming. If you don't have cash in hand, profit means nothing. That's why tracking your money, all of it, matters. Every dollar in, every dollar out. You have to plan for slow seasons before they happen, not when you're already in them. And for the love of caffeine and sanity, don't let your bank balance trick you into thinking you're financially solid. Money sitting in your account today doesn't mean you're in the clear; it just means you haven't paid all your bills yet.

NOT EVERY JOB IS WORTH YOUR TIME

I once asked a contractor:

"What's your best-paying service?"

"We do a little bit of everything."

"Okay, but which jobs make you the most profit?"

(*blinks*).

As the pot in this scenario, I hate to call out the kettle ... and I get it, when business is slow, you'll take almost anything. But some jobs are gold mines and some are money pits.

If you don't track job profitability, you might be doing work that's actually costing you money.

Let's talk about a few of my favorite people.

Scott Hester, Nathan Artman, and Bradley Martin run Asa Carlton, Inc., a national commercial construction company. I've seen Scott, who's a finance whiz, walk away from a multi-million-dollar job because the margin was so razor thin, a few days of rain could wipe out the entire profit.

Commercial construction can be brutal on margins. That decision wasn't about chasing pots of gold; it was about understanding risk and protecting the company.

Here's the short version: they track everything. Sales, marketing, labor hours, bid-to-win ratios, insurance, materials, and execution. They know what it costs to win a job and what it costs to deliver it. That clarity helps them avoid jobs that "look" great but quietly bleed the business dry.

A more down-to-earth example:

One of my electrician clients was awarded a $40,000 commercial lighting contract, an exciting job with sleek designs and unique fixtures. One for the website, for sure.

He tried to be smart:

- His original pricing accounted for labor overages.

- It included material additions.

What he didn't factor in were the delays or the multiple client meetings to discuss changes.

When all was said and done, he lost around $1,000 on the job.

That may not sound like much, but it's a truck payment. It covers part of payroll. And if it happens more than once? It can shake a business to its core.

If you track job profitability, you'll start noticing:

- *"This type of job makes us way more money for less time."*
- *"We're undercharging on service calls and getting killed on labor."*
- *"This 'big' job looks great on paper but pays like crap."*
- *You'll also start to realize the costs that you eat and may not even have a structure to charge for.*

If your jobs aren't profitable, raise your prices or stop doing them.

FINAL THOUGHT: YOU CAN'T "WORK HARDER" OUT OF FINANCIAL CHAOS

If working harder were the answer, most business owners would be millionaires.

But hard work without financial systems is just exhaustion.

And that's why the next chapter matters:

We're going to talk about pricing.

How to stop undercharging.

How to make sure you're not the cheapest person in your market.

Because if you don't price your work right, no amount of financial tracking will save you.

Let's fix that next.

WHAT DADDY WOULD TELL YOU

If my dad were sitting across from you right now, he'd lean forward, rest his forearms on the table, and say, "People first. Always."

And he wouldn't be wrong.

But he'd also tell you something else, something he learned through decades of running a business, something he saw crystal clear by the end: If you don't take care of the business, it can't take care of you.

Because here's the thing, he figured it out. By the time those final years rolled around, he was making more money than ever. He wasn't out there grinding for scraps. He knew how to price his work, how to keep expenses in check, and how to make sure every job actually paid. But what he didn't do?

He didn't put the right systems in place to keep that money coming when he wasn't the one showing up.

It wasn't a lack of discipline or know-how. He ran a debt-free, profitable business and could quote his numbers better than most CFOs. But what he didn't build, because no one told him he needed to, was a business that could survive without him.

And that's the part that broke my heart.

No maintenance contracts. No automated customer outreach. No scalable processes to make money without him physically being there.

Not because he didn't believe in those things, he did. But because, for years, he convinced himself that customers would just call when they needed him. And they did. But when he couldn't answer anymore? The business had nothing left to stand on.

That still stings today.

Not because he failed, he didn't. Not because he didn't work hard enough, he worked harder than anyone I've ever met. But because, at the end, he saw it so clearly. He knew what he could have done differently. And he told me.

So if he were here right now, reading this book, he wouldn't be shaking his head at you. He wouldn't be telling you to grind harder, hustle more, or push yourself to exhaustion.

He'd tell you to take care of your business the way you take care of your customers.

Because your business?

It should take care of YOU, too.

CHAPTER 5
MASTERING THE NUMBERS

HOW FINANCIAL DATA FUELS GROWTH AND LEGACY

It was never about the money, until it was.

Dad never set out to build an empire. He wanted to provide, to take care of his family, to make sure my mom never had to worry. He wasn't chasing millions; he was chasing stability. And for the most part, he found it.

But here's the thing about stability: it's a slippery little devil. It lulls you into thinking everything is fine, until one day, it isn't.

I wish I could tell you that when my dad had his stroke, we had everything in place to seamlessly transition his business, that he had structured it in a way that allowed for someone else to step in, keep things running, and continue serving his customers.

That's not what happened.

Because while my dad had built something incredible, he had built it around himself. His knowledge, his skills, his relationships ... these were the foundation of his success. But none of those things were easily transferable. There was no financial dashboard tracking long-term trends, no organized customer data system, and no plan for how the business could function without him.

And that is where so many small business owners go wrong.

If your business is entirely dependent on you, then it isn't a business. It's a job you've created for yourself.

This chapter isn't just about numbers; it's about power. The power to make decisions based on financial reality rather than guesswork. The power to create something that can grow beyond you. The power to leave behind more than just a great story.

THE ROLE OF A CRM: YOUR BUSINESS'S MEMORY BANK

They say the devil is in the details, but where did you put the details? On a sticky note? In the notes app on your phone? On the back of an old invoice? That's not a system, it's a scavenger hunt. And one lost scrap of paper away from chaos.

Enter Customer Relationship Management (CRM) software. A CRM isn't just a fancy digital Rolodex. It's a powerful tool that helps businesses track customer interactions, manage leads, follow up on sales opportunities, and even predict future revenue.

Think about all the information you try to keep in your head: which customers are due for follow-ups, which jobs are still pending approval, which estimates haven't been accepted. Now imagine if all of that data lived in one place, accessible at a glance.

A CRM can:

- Store customer details (names, emails, phone numbers, service history, preferences, everything in one place).
- Track sales and project pipelines so you know what's booked, what's pending, and what needs attention.
- Automate follow-ups to make sure no opportunity slips through the cracks.
- Provide dashboards and reports that show revenue trends, customer retention rates, and which marketing efforts are actually working.

Without a CRM, you're flying blind. With one, you have instant insight into the lifeblood of your business, your customers, your cash flow, and your future opportunities.

CUSTOMER-CENTRIC FINANCIAL INSIGHTS (A.K.A. STOP GUESSING, START TRACKING)

Your business lives and dies by your customers. They're not just names on checks; they're the whole reason your lights are still on. So why do so many business owners still treat customer data like it's optional?

Let's put it this way:

You wouldn't show up to a job site without your tools.

So why are you making pricing and marketing decisions without knowing *how much your customers are actually worth*?

If you don't know:

- How much it costs to get a new customer
- How long they stick around
- Or how much they spend over time

...then you're basically playing darts in the dark and hoping it hits the board. Spoiler: it doesn't.

And if you're still scribbling names and numbers on napkins or fishing through emails to find phone numbers? Friend. Please.

Start with this:

1. Full name
2. Email (PLEASE GET THIS)
3. Phone number
4. Where they came from (Not from a land called Honalee. Real-world origin story, please. Are they a

referral, ad, or met you at Kroger when they tripped and read your company name on the way down?)

5. What they bought
6. How much they spent

If you're not ready for a full-blown CRM (which we highly recommend), at least set up a Google Sheet and track it like your business depends on it! Because, news flash, cousin Eddie, it does.

This kind of insight helps you stop wasting time on one-and-done customers and start investing in the ones who actually move the needle.

Know your people. Know their patterns. Know your worth.

CAC & CLV: THE HOT MESS AND THE GOLDEN GOOSE

Customer Acquisition Cost (CAC)

CAC = how much it costs you to land a new customer

Simple, right? Until you realize it's not just about the ad spend. It's the emails. The calls. The re-calls. The quote that took two hours and got ghosted. The mental gymnastics of being charming and professional, even when they ask, "Can I get a discount if I pay cash?"

Pro tip: Your time is money. If you're chasing leads like you're on *The Bachelor,* CAC includes *you,* too.

Formula:

CAC = Total Sales + Marketing Costs / Number of New Customers Acquired

Translation: If it's costing you $500 to land a $300 job... congratulations. You're not running a business. You're that guy in the dunk tank at the Little League fundraiser, soaking wet, wondering how you got talked into this, getting hit in the face *and* paying for the privilege.

If it's costing you more to get customers than you're making from them, you're not scaling, you're subsidizing strangers. You're doing all the work, footing the bill, and watching them vanish before the ink dries.

Customer Lifetime Value (CLV)

CLV = how much a customer is actually worth over the long haul.

If CAC is your blind date, CLV is the person who calls you back, brings tacos, and helps you move.

Formula:

CLV = Average Sale × Repeat Purchases × How Long They Stick Around

Translation: If you're in HVAC and your average CLV is $47,000... and you're obsessing over a $200 lead? Get your priorities straight.

Low CLV = one-hit wonder (Think *"Achy Breaky Heart."*)

High CLV = greatest hits album (Think *Lynyrd Skynyrd's Gold & Platinum.* Be *that*.)

WHY THIS ACTUALLY MATTERS (A LOT)

Here's the ratio that makes or breaks your business:

CLV should be at least 3x your CAC.

That means if you're spending $300 to get a customer, they better be worth $900 or more over time. Otherwise? You're buying relationships you can't afford.

My dad? He was the king of customer loyalty.

Did great work. Showed up when he said he would. Charged fair prices. People *loved* him. His Customer Lifetime Value? It was probably through the roof... like HVAC-on-a-roof-unit levels of high.

But the thing is... he never tracked any of it. Not once.

No spreadsheets. No CRM. No sticky notes. Just a man, a

van, and a photographic memory that somehow included every job he'd ever done since the Reagan administration.

All that gold? Locked in his brain like a Rubik's Cube someone Gorilla Glued mid-solve, colorful, brilliant, but frozen in place and impossible to pass on.

You couldn't peel the stickers off, and you sure weren't gonna solve it.

It was *his* system. And without him, well ... we had a van and some tools.

So when it came time to sell? There was nothing to hand off. Just years of goodwill and relationships that lived in one place: his head. Oh, and on some carbonless invoices (we still have stacks of those).

And look, it worked, for him. But if you're building something that *outlives* you, or at least survives a vacation, you've got to get that data out of your skull and into a system someone else can follow. Even if that "system" starts as a Google Sheet named something like "DON'T DELETE THIS."

Moral of the story?

Track this stuff. Know your numbers. Or risk building a business that dies with your calendar and your charm.

PRICING FOR PROFIT

Pricing jobs is where contractors tend to shoot themselves in the foot. Not because they don't know their trade, but because they don't know their numbers. Sometimes they also don't understand their value. And if you're pricing based on labor and materials alone, buckle up, because that's a fast track to broke.

Unless, of course, your business is just a tax shelter ... that's another book that I will never write.

THE BASICS OF PRICING

The biggest mistake? Forgetting overhead. That office (or your basement command center), the admin staff (or you wearing 12 different hats), your fleet of trucks (or your one reliable but ever-rustier truck), the tools, the equipment, the insurance, even the branded shirts you wear, it all costs money. And if you're not factoring those costs into your pricing, guess what? You're paying for your customers to get a deal.

MARKUP ≠ PROFIT

Let's get this straight once and for all: Markup is NOT the same as profit.

If you think adding a 30% markup on materials means you're making 30% profit, you're wrong. That markup covers materials, not your labor, overhead, taxes, or the actual margin you need to stay in business.

Let's say you charge $1000 for a job, and your costs (labor, materials, overhead) total $750. That leaves you with $250 in profit, which sounds great until you remember that you also have to pay taxes, insurance, and reinvest in your business.

You're not making 25% profit. You're barely making ends meet.

THE DANGER OF COMPETING ON PRICE

If your plan is to be the cheapest option, good luck. Someone will always undercut you. Instead, focus on value. People will pay more for reliability, quality, and expertise. If you're setting your prices based on covering costs instead of building wealth, you're playing the wrong game.

HOW A CRM CAN HELP YOU TRACK PROFITABILITY

The numbers aren't just numbers. They tell a story. A story of whether your business is built to last, or just built for today.

A CRM, when used correctly, can help you track real profitability by:

- Monitoring the true cost per customer (not just what you charge them).
- Tracking historical trends in pricing, labor, and materials.
- Sending automated reminders for follow-ups and upsells.
- Allowing quick reporting on which projects were profitable and which ones were not.

THE LEGACY OF A WELL-BUILT BUSINESS

When my dad's business shut down, people still called looking for him. His name carried weight. But his business? Gone.

He built something incredible, but he didn't build it to outlast him.

And that's the difference between a job and a business.

A job pays you while you work.

A business pays you even when you don't.

A job dies when you step away.

A business keeps running.

You get to decide which one you're building.

If I can leave you with a thinking prompt, it's just: what story are you writing?

CHAPTER 6

BUILDING A BUSINESS THAT'S WORTH SOMETHING
THE BEST INTENTIONS DON'T BUILD VALUE

My father Link tried to sell maintenance contracts. He bought into a system, had the paperwork ready, and even managed to sell... about five.

Not because he wasn't good at what he did. Not because his customers didn't need it. But because, at that moment, he didn't feel like bothering people. Maybe it was loyalty, maybe it was fear of rejection, maybe it was just too much of a hassle. Whatever the reason, the opportunity passed him by.

And that's the problem. Intending to build value isn't the same as actually doing it. Something about a road... to a very warm zip code... paved with good intentions? Yeah. That one.

If he had followed through, those contracts could have added predictable revenue and made his business more valuable when he stepped away. But like so many business owners, he figured he'd get around to it eventually. He never did.

Link didn't wake up one day and decide not to build a more valuable business. He just kept pushing things to tomorrow until tomorrow ran out. If I could go back in time and ask him if he would do things differently, I think I know what he would say. Not because he ever admitted to regretting much, but because I know how much he wanted to make sure my mother was taken care of. He wanted to leave behind more than memories and old invoices. He wanted to build something that lasted. And that's what most business owners want, until the reality of day-to-day operations keeps them from seeing the bigger picture.

A business's value isn't just about revenue; it's about how well it runs without you.

LARRY CAN FIX ANYTHING, EXCEPT HIS CALENDAR

Larry is an electrician turned custom home builder. The kind of guy who can trace a dead neutral across three breaker boxes and a mystery junction no one else could find, but still has to check his voicemail to remember which house he was supposed to be at an hour ago. He built his company from the ground up, powered by grit, raw talent, and the belief that if you did great work, everything else would sort itself out.

For a while, that felt true. Business was booming, customers were happy, and Larry had enough work to keep him going six days a week. But the cracks started to show. He was drowning in paperwork, chasing invoices as fast as a teenager late for curfew, and spending more time putting out fires than building anything. His wife Jan, who handled the books, was losing patience... and sleep.

That's when he had his first real encounter with the dreaded "computer mess".

LARRY VS. THE SAVE BUTTON

Larry sat at the kitchen table, staring at his laptop like it was a ticking time bomb. Jan stood over his shoulder, arms crossed, watching him with the patience of a woman who had seen this movie too many times.

"Just click it," she said.

Larry shook his head. "I don't trust it."

Jan rolled her eyes. "It's a scheduling system, not a government conspiracy. Just click the damn button."

Larry, a man who had once scaled 50-foot electrical poles without breaking a sweat, hovered his mouse over the 'Save' button like it might explode. "What if it screws up my jobs? What if I can't find my notes? What if it starts running my life?"

Jan took a deep breath and leaned in. "Larry, your *life* is already running *you*; you just don't have a system tracking it. Now hit Save."

With the hesitancy of a man agreeing to saw off his own arm, Larry clicked. The screen blinked. The job was saved. The world didn't end.

Larry sat back. "Huh. That wasn't so bad."

Jan smirked. "You think?"

The truth was, Larry had been running his business like a firehouse, constantly dowsing the flames, running from one emergency to another. His days were spent fixing problems, handling last-minute changes, and barely keeping up with paperwork. But once he embraced systems, everything changed.

His crew knew where they were supposed to be without him calling ten times a day. Clients got automatic updates. Invoices went out on time. And most importantly ... Larry got some of his sanity back.

The hardest part about adopting systems isn't using them. It's admitting you need them.

LARRY DOES THE MATH (AND DRAMATICALLY COMPLAINS ABOUT IT)

A few months into using his fancy new systems, Larry and Jan sat down to look at the numbers.

"So," Larry said, arms crossed, "how much did all this cost us?"

Jan tapped on her tablet, scrolling through their expenses. "Between the software, setup, and training? About twenty grand."

Larry nearly choked on his coffee. "TWENTY THOU-SAND DOLLARS? Jan, I could have bought a fishing boat!"

Jan didn't even look up. "You don't fish, Larry."

"I *could* have started!"

Jan slid the tablet across the table. "Look at the numbers before you have a heart attack."

Larry grumbled, but actually looked. And for the first time, he saw it:

- Their revenue was up 20% because they were finishing jobs faster.
- Their expenses were down because they weren't double-ordering materials.
- They were getting paid on time because invoices weren't slipping through the cracks.
- And best of all? Larry was home for dinner most nights.

Larry exhaled and rubbed his temples. "So what you're telling me is... I fought this for nothing?"

Jan smirked. "Oh no. Watching you lose your mind? Totally worth it."

WHAT BUSINESS OWNERS NEED TO DO TO BUILD VALUE

- Document Your Processes: If it's all in your head, it's worthless to anyone else. Write it down.
- Embrace Systems: Scheduling, invoicing, project management, use tools that make your life easier.
- Create Recurring Revenue: Maintenance contracts, subscriptions, or long-term agreements increase value.
- Delegate: If you're the only one who can do something, you've built a bottleneck, not a business.
- Track Financials Like a Business, Not a Hobby: Know your margins, cash flow, and forecast.
- Think About the Future Now: If you want to sell, retire, or even take a real vacation, start preparing.
- Document Customer Information Religiously: If you can't contact everyone easily, you're not ready.

The lesson? Most business owners fight systems because they're afraid of losing control. But the truth is, systems are what give you control. They stop the chaos. They free you from micromanagement. And if you do it right, they make your business more valuable, whether you keep it or sell it.

Larry may not have gotten his fishing boat, but he got something better: a business that runs smoothly without him at the center of every single thing.

And if he ever *does* want to sell?

He now has something a buyer would actually want.

The real question is: What's stopping you from doing the same?

CHAPTER 7
A MESSAGE TO BUSINESS OWNERS
THE TRUE VALUE OF OPERATIONAL EFFICIENCY

EFFORT ISN'T THE SAME AS EFFICIENCY

Running a business without efficient operations is like getting a flat tire and seriously considering wrapping your spare in electrical tape.

Hear me out.

I had a flat the other day, and a man named Guy—yes, *a guy named Guy*—offered to help. Turns out my spare also had a screw in it (because of course it did), and without hesitation, Guy grabbed a roll of electrical tape and went to work. He wrapped that tire like it was a holiday ham and said,

"This should hold long enough to get you where you're going."

Now, I knew better. I smiled, thanked him politely, and then gratefully accepted help from another good Samaritan named Mark, who helped me haul the actual tire across the parking lot to the Walmart tire center so it could be properly fixed.

You can smile, nod, and pretend duct tape (or electrical, if it's all you've got) and a dream will get you where you're going, but deep down, you know better.

Electrical tape on a tire isn't a temporary fix. It's a delusion.

It *looks* like effort. It *feels* like motion. But it's not getting you anywhere that lasts.

Bless his heart.

What you really need are systems. A plan. And someone like Mark. Someone who's willing to roll the heavy thing with you, all the way to the place where it gets truly fixed.

On with the story...

A TALE OF TWO SERVICE PROVIDERS

Meet Jack and Sarah, two service providers in the plumbing and electrical industries. While both were incredibly skilled in their own ways, their approaches to running their businesses couldn't have been more different.

JACK'S STRUGGLE WITH OPERATIONS

Jack was an incredible electrician, the kind of guy who could walk into a flickering room, sniff the drywall, and know which junction box had a loose connection. His customers loved him. He was personable, skilled, and dependable... when he showed up.

But *running* the business? That was a different story.

Jack's scheduling "system" lived entirely in his head and on the back of old receipts. He regularly double-booked himself or missed appointments entirely. Half the time, he was making emergency runs to the supply house because he'd forgotten something basic. The other half, he was stuck in his van, digging through tools to find a meter he swore he had yesterday.

Invoicing? A comedy of errors. Sometimes he undercharged by hundreds. Other times, he forgot to bill at all. His work van looked like a RES location exploded inside it (because, it kinda did), and despite working 12-hour days, he was always behind.

When his wife gently suggested they think about selling the business and finally retiring, Jack got quiet.

He had no idea what the business was worth.

And worse? He realized it *wasn't* a business; without him, there was nothing to sell. No systems, no structure, no repeatable value. Just a man, a van, and a lifetime of hustle that couldn't be handed off.

SARAH'S OPERATIONAL TURNAROUND

In contrast to Jack's chaotic business, Sarah inherited a plumbing company and took a systematic approach to transform its operations.

Sarah's story began differently. She inherited her father, Ronald's, plumbing business after his unexpected passing, believing she was stepping into a well-oiled machine. Instead, she found a mess, outdated records, disorganized inventory, and employees who were great at their trade but had no clear system for managing jobs.

Sarah, who had a background in business management but no experience in plumbing, knew she had to get things under control fast. Otherwise, she'd have to close the doors. She started by investing in business management software that centralized all customer data, service history, and scheduling. Instead of relying on memory or sticky notes, everything was now logged in a system that made sense.

She standardized pricing, implemented digital invoicing, and developed a restocking system for the company vehicles to ensure that every technician had what they needed before heading to a job. She also introduced key performance indicators (KPIs) to track revenue per technician, customer satisfaction, and average job completion time.

Sarah's employees were not thrilled with the changes.

In fact, they were downright hostile.

"We've always done it this way," grumbled Jim, her lead technician, crossing his arms. "I don't see why we need some fancy new system to tell us what we already know."

Sarah resisted the urge to point out that what they already knew had them constantly scrambling for parts, showing up to the wrong job sites, and working 60-hour weeks just to break even.

Instead, she smiled sweetly. "Oh, no worries, Jim. If you prefer, I can keep calling you at 9 p.m. when I find out you didn't submit your job notes, so we have no idea what to charge the customer."

Jim scowled. The others chuckled.

For the first few weeks, it was like herding cats. Some employees "forgot" to enter data. Others flat-out refused, claiming it was "too complicated." The scheduling app went ignored, and old habits crept back in.

Sarah knew she had to get creative. So she made a bet.

"If we do this my way for six months, and you don't make more money," she announced one morning, "I will personally dress up as Dolly Parton and ride on the company float in the Fourth of July parade."

Silence.

Then, laughter.

"You?" Jim smirked. "In a wig? And, what, balloo ... um, high heels?"

"You better believe it. The whole get-up, wig, rhinestones, a microphone for some backup singing," she shot back. "But if you do make more money, we turn that into a profit-sharing system. Your hard work earns you more."

Jim squinted at her. "Wait... do I have to dress up like Dolly if we do make more money?"

Sarah considered it. "Only if you sabotage the system to make me lose."

The crew erupted into laughter.

From then on, the employees reluctantly, then enthusiastically, embraced the new systems. As months passed, the data proved Sarah right. Jobs were getting done faster. Fewer mistakes were made. And everyone, *everyone*, was making more money.

By the time summer rolled around, the entire crew was singing Jolene in the breakroom, because not only had Sarah won the bet, but they were making 20% more annually.

No Dolly Parton float required.

THE DIFFERENCE BETWEEN OPERATIONS AND DELIVERY

Too often, business owners confuse *doing the work* with *running the business*. But they aren't the same thing.

- Service Delivery is the actual work you do for customers. Jack was incredible at this part, but it wasn't enough.
- Operations are everything behind the scenes that make service delivery happen smoothly: scheduling, invoicing, customer management, and inventory tracking. Sarah figured out that without this, her father's business was on the brink of collapse.

Many small business owners pour everything into *service delivery* and neglect *operations*. But as Jack discovered, being great at what you do doesn't make your business valuable.

And as Sarah proved, fixing operations can turn a business from barely surviving into something thriving, efficient, and valuable.

WHY OPERATIONAL EFFICIENCY MATTERS

- Increased Productivity: Sarah's team could complete more jobs in less time.
- Improved Customer Satisfaction: Easy scheduling, clear communication, and accurate invoicing kept clients happy.
- Reduced Stress: No more constant fire drills, Sarah and her team could finally breathe.
- Better Financial Management: With clean records and tracking, Sarah made smarter decisions.
- Business Value: The company could run without her. That's value you can sell, or step away from.

STEPS TO IMPROVE YOUR OPERATIONAL EFFICIENCY

- Invest in Technology: Use tools for scheduling, invoicing, and managing customers.
- Standardize Your Processes: Create consistency so no one's winging it.
- Organize Equipment & Inventory: Stop wasting time searching for parts.
- Implement a Customer Management System: Don't rely on memory, track it all.
- Refine Pricing & Invoicing: Bill accurately, consistently, and on time.
- Commit to Continual Improvement: Small changes stack up into big wins.

THE LEGACY YOU'RE BUILDING

Remember Link's story from earlier in the book? He had the skill, the reputation, and the loyal customers, but no transferable value. His business, built on his back, couldn't survive without him.

Sarah refused to let that happen to her father's business. By focusing on operational efficiency, she didn't just make life easier; she built a business that could *outlive her*. Whether she sells it, franchises it, or passes it down, her father's legacy will continue.

It was possible only because she turned chaos into structure. And structure? That's what legacy is made of.

Action Steps: Build a Strong Operations Backbone

1. Assess Your Current Operations: Where are you losing time, money, or momentum?
2. Choose One Area to Improve: Don't try to fix everything at once, pick one priority, and then pick another one after that.
3. Invest in a Tool or System: Even a simple CRM, scheduling app, or inventory tracker can change everything.
4. Document Your Processes: Make your business learnable. Repeatable. Transferable.
5. Review and Refine Regularly: Efficiency is not a one-time fix. It's a habit.

AND HERE'S THE TRUTH

Building a business with transferable value isn't just about making life easier today; it's about ensuring that when the time comes, your business can stand on its own... with or without you.

Whether you plan to retire, sell, or scale, it all starts here: Running an efficient operation.

So the real question isn't just:

How good are you at your trade?

It's:

How good is your business at running itself?

In the next chapter, we'll talk about how to maintain your standards as you scale, without staying stuck as the only one who can "do it right."

CHAPTER 8

BUILDING QUALITY INTO YOUR BUSINESS
SO YOU CAN LET GO WITHOUT LOSING YOUR MIND

If you ever want to scale your business without losing your mind or your reputation, you need quality assurance (QA).

QA is what separates *you doing the work* from *your business doing the work.*

A lot of owners get stuck here. They think they're the only ones who can do things the right way, and honestly, they might be right, for now. But without systems to ensure consistent quality, you've just built a really stressful job with your name on it.

Jack, from earlier? Brilliant electrician. But without QA, his business was a chaotic one-man show, held together with grit and guesswork.

Sarah? She figured it out. She realized that if she wanted her dad's business to outlive her, she couldn't be the only one holding the standard. She needed a system anyone could follow and everyone could trust.

WHAT QA ACTUALLY DOES FOR YOU

Quality assurance isn't about perfection. It's about predictability.

It gives your customers confidence.

It gives your employees clarity.

And it gives you the ability to step away without everything falling apart.

Without it, you get:

- Mixed results
- Sloppy work
- Angry reviews
- And good employees quitting because they're tired of figuring things out on their own

HOW TO BUILD QUALITY INTO YOUR OPERATIONS

Here's how to bake QA into your systems without turning it into a corporate nightmare:

- Standard Operating Procedures (SOPs):

If it's only in your head, it's a liability. Write it down. Record a walkthrough. Make it repeatable.

- Ongoing Training: Training isn't a one-and-done. Reinforce what good work looks like. People forget. That's human.
- Checklists and Workflow Tools: Pilots use checklists. So do surgeons. You should, too.
- Customer Feedback and Internal Reviews: Don't wait for an angry customer to tell you what went wrong. Build in checkpoints. Ask. Review. Adjust.

WHY THIS REALLY MATTERS

Quality assurance isn't about control. It's about trust.

It protects your reputation when you're not in the room.

It frees up your time without lowering your standards.

And it turns your business into something that lasts, whether you're there or not.

HIRING THE RIGHT PEOPLE

Sarah didn't build a smoother business by accident; she hired the right people and trained them to thrive inside a system. If you want consistency and growth, you need more than warm bodies and basic resumes. You need people who elevate the work, not just execute it.

Hiring should never be about finding someone who just "follows directions." You're not building a factory floor, you're building a team. The best business owners aren't afraid to hire people who are better than they are in specific areas.

If you own a painting business, hire the guy who cuts cleaner corners. If you run HVAC, don't be threatened by the tech who can diagnose a heat pump with his eyes closed. That's not a threat, it's strength. When your team gets better, your company gets stronger.

And when it comes to roles outside your trade? Stop pretending you can wear every hat.

- Bookkeeping: Financial chaos will sink you faster than bad reviews. Whether it's in-house or outsourced, get professional help.
- Marketing: Your reputation matters, but visibility pays the bills. If you don't market well, you'll always be playing catch-up.

- Cybersecurity and IT: If your customer database lives in an unprotected spreadsheet, you're one phishing email away from disaster. Lock it down.

TRAINING PROGRAMS AND APPRENTICESHIPS

If you want to scale without losing your edge, training isn't optional. It's how you protect your standards.

- Apprenticeships let you grow future leaders from within. Teach the next generation not just how to do the work, but how to do it *your way*.
- Ongoing internal training keeps your standards high and your team sharp.
- Mentorship builds loyalty, closes skill gaps, and creates a team that supports each other without depending on you for every answer.

WHEN TO BUILD IN-HOUSE TEAMS

In the beginning, outsourcing is smart. It's lean, it's flexible, and it gets the job done. But as your business grows, some roles need to come home.

- Do a cost-benefit analysis to see when it's cheaper and smarter to bring someone on full-time.
- Prioritize roles that impact the customer experience. A bad IT call center won't tank your brand, but a bad project manager will.
- Invest in leadership. An in-house team without strong leadership is just a group of people doing tasks. You need people who lead by example and reinforce your standards every day.

BAKING QA INTO DAILY OPERATIONS

A solid business runs on two tracks: operational efficiency and quality assurance. One without the other is like brakes without steering.

Here's how to make QA part of the rhythm, not just a report:

- Standardize workflows so every task follows a repeatable process.
- Automate where it makes sense: Remove human error where you can, and simplify the rest.
- Set performance metrics and actually track them. What gets measured gets managed.
- Build ownership into your culture: Great QA isn't about policing, it's about pride.
- Establish feedback loops: QA isn't a one-and-done. It's a habit.

FINAL THOUGHTS: THE POWER OF LETTING GO

Scaling a business doesn't mean cloning yourself. It means building systems that work *without* you constantly hovering. That's not laziness, it's leadership.

When you integrate QA into your daily operations, you protect your customer experience, your team, and your peace of mind. More importantly, you create something that lasts. Something that can grow, adapt, and even change hands, without falling apart.

That's what real value looks like.

So here's the question to close this chapter:

Are you building a business that depends on you, or one that could outlive you?

CHAPTER 9
FROM SATISFACTION TO LOYALTY
THE PINNACLE OF CUSTOMER SUCCESS

In service-based businesses, "customer satisfaction" gets tossed around like it's the finish line. Did the customer pay? Are they not yelling? Great! Call it a win.

But that's not loyalty. That's silence.

Loyalty is when someone tells ten people about you. It's when they won't let their cousin call *anyone else*. It's when they defend you on Facebook like you're blood.

That kind of loyalty doesn't come from doing the bare minimum. It comes from going deeper. Showing up. Solving problems no one else will touch. Treating their home or business like it's your own.

My dad, Link Helmandollar, had no shortage of loyal customers. But few stuck with him like the Stephens did.

THE STEPHENS' SCHOOLHOUSE SUCCESS

Charles and June Stephens purchased an old two-room schoolhouse, thinking they could preserve history and turn the building into a cozy lakeside retreat. What they actually bought was a crumbling rock foundation with interior walls full of ivy, questionable structural integrity, and electrical wiring so outdated it likely predated *electricians*. This wasn't just old-school wiring, it was *first-generation* wiring. The kind that made you wonder if the original installer had read about electricity in a newspaper once and thought, *yeah, I can probably figure that out.*

Enter Link.

Where most contractors saw an expensive demolition project, Link saw *potential*. He saw the headaches too, and he was very clear with the Stephens what it was going to take to turn a ramshackle building into a home.

Over months, he painstakingly restored the schoolhouse, reinforcing the foundation, replacing beams, and evicting the ivy like a no-nonsense landlord. He didn't just make the structure sound, he made it beautiful.

When it was finished, the schoolhouse was restored, unrecognizable (unless you were native to the area and over the age of 70), transformed into a stunning lakeside home. The Stephens were thrilled. They told everyone about their "miracle-working" contractor and swore they'd never use anyone else.

THE LOYALTY FORMULA: WHY CUSTOMERS STICK AROUND

The Stephens weren't just fans of Link's craftsmanship. They stuck with him because of three essential qualities:

1. Trust & Communication

Link didn't just show up and start hammering. He kept the Stephens informed every step of the way. He answered calls, explained processes, and was transparent about costs and timelines.

2. Consistent Excellence

Every beam, every nail, every shingle, Link treated every part of the job with the same level of care. The Stephens never had to wonder if he'd cut corners.

3. Emotional Connection

This isn't about "friending" your clients on Facebook, it's about *understanding their vision* and treating their home like it's your own. Link cared about their project, and they knew it.

When customers trust you, believe in your quality, and feel valued, they don't just stick around. They become your best marketing team.

THE POWER OF REFERRALS

Here's the thing about loyal customers: *they talk.*

The Stephens didn't just call Link for their own projects; they sent their friends, family, and neighbors to him, too. Why? Because when you find a service provider you love, you *want* the people you care about to have the same great experience.

Link didn't need flashy marketing campaigns. His business grew because his happy customers became his most powerful (and free) sales force.

Pro Tip: If your customers *aren't* referring you, ask yourself: *Would I recommend my own business if I were them?*

HOW TO MEASURE CUSTOMER LOYALTY (WITHOUT JUST GUESSING)

Loyal customers are easy to spot:

They come back without being begged.

They send their friends your way.

They'll wait for you instead of Googling someone new.

But if you're only measuring loyalty by who's still texting you, you're leaving money, and insight on the table.

To build real loyalty (the kind that makes your business recession-proof), you have to understand what your customers care about, not just what they buy.

THE PSYCHOLOGY BEHIND LOYALTY

People don't make purchasing decisions the way we think they do.

They're not spreadsheets with legs. They're emotional creatures with habits, triggers, and gut-level instincts.

As Robert Manigold, Head of Strategic Partnerships at PROOF Positioning, puts it:

"We don't buy based on logic. We buy based on what feels right, then we go looking for reasons to back it up. If you want loyal customers, you have to connect with what matters to them below the surface."

That means understanding not just what they say they want, but what actually drives their behavior. That's where tools like market research and behavioral economics come in. These aren't academic theories; they're the practical keys to becoming your customer's first call, every time.

WANT TO KNOW IF YOU'RE GETTING LOYALTY RIGHT? TRY THIS.

1. Ask Better Questions

Don't just ask "Were you satisfied?"

Ask: "What almost made you choose someone else?" or "What made you feel most confident about hiring us?"

That's where the gold is.

2. Track Repeat Business & Referrals

Referrals are the applause of small business.

If no one's clapping, check your performance.

3. Notice What They Don't Say

Are they hesitating before signing off? Ghosting after the job? Seeming relieved when it's done?

That's customer feedback, too, it just doesn't come with a survey.

DON'T JUST SERVE CUSTOMERS. STUDY THEM.

You don't need to be creepy or corporate. You just need to *care enough to look closer*.

When you understand what truly makes your customers tick… and stick… you stop playing defense with your marketing. You start building a brand that they trust without question.

That's not just loyalty. That's leverage.

CULTIVATING A LOYAL CUSTOMER BASE

You don't get loyalty just because you do a decent job. You earn it. Here's how:

1. Actually Listen to Your Customers

Don't assume you know what they want; ask them.

2. Adapt Quickly

If customers are *consistently* asking for something you don't offer, maybe it's time to start.

3. Stay in Touch

Send updates, holiday messages, or reminders when their service is due. (A "Hey, it's been a year since we … *insert the last service!*" email goes a long way.)

4. Be Ridiculously Consistent

Customers trust businesses that *always* deliver high-quality service, not just when they feel like it.

5. Celebrate the Relationship

Remember their milestones, anniversaries of service, birthdays, or just a simple thank-you. It shows you value them beyond their wallet.

THE LEGACY OF LOYALTY

People still speak Link's name with admiration. His old phone still rings with customers who wish they could hire him one more time. That's legacy-level loyalty.

And that's what you should aim for.

Your business shouldn't just be a place customers go because it's convenient. It should be the *only* place they want to go.

Because when loyalty is built into your business model, you don't just create revenue, you create something *that lasts*.

PREMIER LOYALTY: A LEGACY OF REPEAT BUSINESS

Loyal customers aren't just happy customers; they're the ones who come back, year after year, even when there are *cheaper* or *faster* options on the market.

Take Premier Building Systems, for example. My client and friend, Scott Philips, started the company 30 years ago, after a supplier he worked with suggested he branch out on his own. He knew how to sell, and he was *meticulous* about follow-ups; he never let a lead go cold. But beyond his natural sales ability, Scott had two secret weapons that built Premier into a powerhouse in the pre-engineered metal building industry:

- He documented everything. Every project, every transaction, every customer relationship, Premier has systems in place to track their work, making sure no detail is left to chance.
- He cultivated loyalty. Even in a *highly competitive* market, Scott has repeat customers who return year

after year because they trust his expertise, his team's reliability, and the consistency of their results.

Scott would tell you he learned trial by fire, but the truth is, he built a business that people want to work with, not just once, but over and over. His attention to numbers has been a key driver in making smart, data-backed business decisions that keep customers coming back.

(He also roots for Clemson. I neither understand nor condone it, but I guess nobody's perfect.)

That's the difference between being a vendor and becoming an indispensable partner.

Loyalty isn't luck. It's built on trust, consistency, and long-term relationships. When you get those things right, like Scott has, your business can thrive for decades.

ACTION STEPS: ASSESS & STRENGTHEN YOUR CUSTOMER LOYALTY

1. Identify Your Best Customers – Who comes back again and again? Why?
2. Examine What's Working – What keeps them loyal? What could you do even better?
3. Recognize Your Problem Customers – Who never seems happy? What can you learn from them?
4. Turn Negative Experiences into Wins – How can you *fix* mistakes and earn back trust?

FINAL THOUGHT: THE LOYALTY TEST

Imagine you had to shut your business down for six months.

Would your customers wait for you? Or would they immediately call your competition?

If the answer makes you nervous, it's time to get to work.

Loyal customers don't just help you survive. They make your business unstoppable.

CHAPTER 10
RISK, RESILIENCE, AND THE ART OF NOT LOSING YOUR SHIRT

Let's be honest, running a service-based business is a bit like riding a rollercoaster blindfolded. You've got the ups, the downs, the unexpected turns, and just when you think you're cruising, something *jolts* you sideways: an economic downturn, a lawsuit, a truck breaking down mid-job with a fully loaded trailer.

The only certainty in business is that uncertainty is inevitable. Read that again.

Link learned this lesson the hard way. When he had his stroke, the business, his *life's work*, collapsed overnight. Not because he wasn't skilled. Not because he wasn't successful. But because there was no contingency plan in place. No system that allowed it to function without him at the helm. His business, like so many others, wasn't built to withstand the unexpected.

And that's where risk management comes in.

THE BUSINESS RISK BUFFET: A LITTLE BIT OF EVERYTHING

Service-based businesses have a smorgasbord of risks, and you don't get to pick just one. It's an all-you-can-eat buffet of potential disasters:

- Operational Risks: Your lead technician calls out sick. Your inventory is mismanaged, and now you have six months' worth of PVC pipe but *no* fittings.
- Financial Risks: Cash flow gets tight. Customers "forget" to pay. The cost of materials jumps 30% overnight because of supply chain issues or tariffs.
- Legal & Regulatory Risks: A licensing requirement changes, and suddenly, your permit to operate is at risk.
- Reputation Risks: One bad review turns into a wildfire.
- Human Resource Risks: Your best employee gets poached. Your worst employee *won't* leave.
- Technology Risks: Your entire customer database disappears because Jim thought clicking that "FREE IPAD" pop-up was a *great* idea.
- Market Risks: The economy dips, interest rates rise, and suddenly no one wants to spend money on non-essential services.

Each of these alone can send a business reeling. Together? They're like an unruly group of toddlers on a sugar high; you need a plan to contain them, or they'll run wild and wreck everything.

HOW TO BUILD A BUSINESS THAT WON'T CRUMBLE UNDER PRESSURE

STEP 1: IDENTIFY YOUR RISKS, BEFORE THEY IDENTIFY YOU

You know that feeling when you hear a weird noise in your truck, but you turn the radio up instead of investigating? That's how most business owners treat risk.

Instead of ignoring problems, do a risk assessment:

- What could go wrong?
- How likely is it?
- What would the impact be?

If a minor annoyance (like a supply chain delay) could turn into a full-blown catastrophe (you have zero inventory for three months), then you need a plan.

STEP 2: PLUG THE HOLES BEFORE THE FLOOD

Once you know your biggest risks, take action. A few smart strategies can mean the difference between a minor hiccup and a business-ending disaster.

Meet Sarah, again.

Remember Sarah, the plumber who inherited her dad's chaotic business? Well, she learned the hard way about risk when an economic downturn nearly wiped her out. Most of her big commercial clients hit the brakes on new projects, and suddenly, she was staring at empty job schedules and mounting bills.

Did she panic? Well, yeah ... a little. But then she pivoted.

- Diversified Her Services: Instead of relying solely on commercial work, Sarah expanded into residential plumbing and emergency services. Burst pipes and clogged drains don't care about economic downturns.
- Built a Cash Reserve: No more running on fumes. She set aside money during busy seasons so she wasn't blindsided when things slowed down.
- Invested in Stronger Tech: She upgraded her scheduling system, optimized her job costing, and implemented a CRM to track leads and follow-ups, so she never lost a warm lead again.
- Cross-Trained Her Team: Her commercial guys learned to handle more residential calls. She made sure she *never* had all her eggs in one basket.
- Developed Multiple Supplier Relationships: When her usual supplier ran out of key materials, she had backup vendors ready to go

Within a year, her business wasn't just surviving, it was thriving.

STEP 3: BUILD RESILIENCE (A.K.A. THE ABILITY TO TAKE A PUNCH AND KEEP GOING)

If risk management is about avoiding disasters, then resilience is about bouncing back when disaster strikes anyway.

A few ways to build business resilience:

- Financial Reserves: Can you keep the lights on for a few months if everything grinds to a halt?
- Flexible Operations: Can you pivot if demand shifts?
- Strong Industry Relationships: Do you have a network to lean on when times get tough?

- Adaptability: Can you change strategies without falling apart?

Sarah's business came out of its downturn stronger because she adapted quickly. Link's, on the other hand, didn't have the foundation to survive when the unexpected happened.

STEP 4: GET YOUR TEAM ON BOARD (BECAUSE THEY'LL MAKE OR BREAK THIS PLAN)

Let's talk about Jim, our guy who clicked the scam pop-up and nearly took the business down with him.

Here's the thing: if your team doesn't understand the importance of risk management, it doesn't matter how good your plan is.

1. Train your employees on basic cybersecurity (A.K.A. *Don't click weird links*).
2. Standardize job site safety protocols so accidents don't lead to lawsuits.
3. Teach your crew how to handle customer complaints before they turn into PR disasters.
4. Make risk management part of the culture, not just a one-time conversation

STEP 5: REVIEW AND REFINE (BECAUSE WHAT WORKS TODAY MIGHT NOT WORK TOMORROW)

Markets shift. New risks emerge. Technology changes. If you don't update your risk management plan regularly, it will become outdated fast.

THE BOTTOM LINE: CONTROL WHAT YOU CAN, PREPARE FOR WHAT YOU CAN'T

Risk can't be eliminated, but it *can* be managed.

If you run your business like Jack, flying by the seat of your pants, hoping nothing goes wrong, then sooner or later, something will.

If you run your business like Sarah, preparing for risks before they happen, you're not just protecting what you've built; you're making it stronger.

THINKING PROMPT: IS YOUR BUSINESS READY FOR THE UNEXPECTED?

Take a few minutes to reflect:

1. What are the three biggest risks to your business right now?
2. If one of those risks became reality tomorrow, how prepared would you be?
3. What's one thing you can do this month to strengthen your business's resilience?

Business is unpredictable. But the difference between success and failure is preparation. So, are you ready for the next curveball?

And once you've earned that loyalty? Protect it. Because risk doesn't go away, it just shifts. And how you handle it will determine whether loyalty sticks... or slips.

CHAPTER 11
WORKFORCE MANAGEMENT

BUILDING A STRONG FOUNDATION FOR THE FUTURE

In case you haven't noticed, we have a problem. A *big* one.

The construction and service industries, including HVAC, electrical, plumbing, commercial, and residential construction, are facing a workforce crisis of epic proportions. It's not coming. It's already here.

THE WORKFORCE SHORTAGE: A CRISIS AND AN OPPORTUNITY

Let's talk numbers:

1. The construction industry needs 546,000 additional workers on top of the usual hiring pace just to meet demand in 2025.
2. 40% of the skilled workforce is over 45 years old, meaning that retirement is on the horizon for a huge portion of the industry.
3. Fewer young people are entering the trades because *someone* convinced them that sitting at a desk all day

answering emails was somehow *better* than making a great living in a trade.

It's a crisis, but it's also an opportunity. Because in a world where supply and demand drive everything, businesses that figure out *how* to attract, train, and retain talent will be the ones that thrive while everyone else scrambles.

THE WAR ON DEI AND WHY IT'S BAD FOR BUSINESS

TRIGGER WARNING (but the good kind):

Before you roll your eyes so hard you see your own spine, let's slow down for a second and talk about what DEI *actually* is, and why it's been turned into such a mess.

Diversity, Equity, and Inclusion (DEI) has become one of those phrases that instantly makes people brace for a lecture or roll into a defensive crouch.

You've probably seen the stereotypes:

- Forced hiring quotas
- Rainbow-washed mission statements
- Awkward corporate emails that say "we value inclusivity" and then do... absolutely nothing

But let's be clear:

DEI, at its core, is just Equal Opportunity Employment with a modern vocabulary.

It's the idea that you should hire based on ability, not skin color, zip code, disability status, or whether someone looks like they walked out of a job site calendar from 1996.

It's not about "checking boxes" or "lowering standards."

It's about not *accidentally* shutting out entire groups of qualified, hardworking people because your business never even thought to look beyond what's familiar.

> *"Diversity work isn't about hiring people to meet a quota, it's about not missing out on great talent because you're stuck on outdated ideas of what 'qualified' looks like. When you broaden your perspective, you strengthen your team."*
>
> - Dr. Vonetta Thompson, Director of HR, Asa Carlton, Inc.

SO, HOW DID DEI BECOME A POLITICAL FOOTBALL?

Like a lot of things in America, DEI got scooped up and spun into something it was never meant to be.

For some, it became a culture war buzzword. For others, a mandatory HR seminar.

The result? Confusion. Frustration. Polarization. And business owners caught in the middle, just trying to build strong teams and keep the lights on.

If you're right-leaning, you're not alone in feeling wary of how DEI has been used, or misused. You're also not wrong to want hiring to be based on merit and fit. That's what most business owners want, regardless of politics.

And if you're left-leaning, you may feel DEI hasn't gone far enough, or that it's been watered down into meaningless gestures. You're not wrong either. When DEI becomes a box to check instead of a strategy to build stronger, more resilient teams, nobody wins.

At the end of the day, good DEI isn't about leaning left or right, it's about looking deeper. It's about asking, *Are we casting the widest net to find the best people? Are we building a workplace where good people want to stay?*

That's not politics. That's leadership.

The good news is: That's what DEI is actually about.

When it's done right, DEI helps you:

- Find great talent you might otherwise overlook
- Build teams that can relate to more customers
- Tap into the loyalty of workers who often feel ignored
- Strengthen your business culture with real-world perspectives

It's not about politics. It's about people. And it's about building a company that lasts.

Bottom line: You don't need a DEI "program" to benefit from what it really stands for; You just need to be intentional about your hiring, your team culture, and the way you support people who show up and do the work.

That's not woke.

That' just smart business.

SO WHAT DOES DEI ACTUALLY REPRESENT?

- Women in Construction (because, surprise, women can run equipment too, and sometimes better than that guy who still can't parallel park).
- Veterans transitioning into civilian careers (because discipline, work ethic, and leadership are kind of a big deal at a job site, not just war zones).
- People with disabilities (who can contribute in massive ways with the right accommodations, plus, they're often the most resourceful people you'll ever meet).
- Second-chance employees (yes, an ex-con can absolutely dig a trench better than your cousin Chad, who still lives in his mom's basement playing Call of Duty).
- Young people (who just need someone to show them that working in the trades is way more lucrative than becoming an influencer who reviews wildly expensive pastries on TikTok).

DEI is about building a workforce that reflects reality. You know, the actual world we live in, not some outdated 1950s sitcom version of it.

HOW TO FIX THE WORKFORCE PROBLEM BEFORE IT'S TOO LATE

If you're a business owner in this industry, here's the harsh truth: You cannot afford to sit back and hope the next generation just magically appears at your doorstep with work boots and a tool belt. The workforce isn't something you just inherit. It's something you build intentionally. Otherwise, you'll be standing in an empty job site, giving yourself the employee of the month award, every month.

Embrace the future, or watch your industry shrink faster than your patience at a four-hour HR seminar.

STEP 1: START EARLY, TRAIN, DON'T JUST HIRE

The reality is, we need to grow talent from within. The days of posting a job ad and getting 30 qualified applicants are over.

Here's how to fix that:

- Apprenticeship Programs → Stop waiting for perfect employees to walk through the door. Train them. Create structured programs that turn entry-level workers into masters of their craft.
- Partnerships with Schools → Work with vocational schools, trade schools, and community colleges to bring in young talent *before* they choose another career.
- In-House Training Programs → If major electrical companies can run their own training schools, why can't small and mid-sized businesses do the same? A well-trained employee is more valuable than a desperate hire.

STEP 2: MODERNIZE THE PERCEPTION OF THE TRADES

Right now, too many people think of plumbing, HVAC, and construction as fallback careers, something you do if "college doesn't work out."

Let's be clear:

- The average electrician makes more than the average college graduate.
- Skilled HVAC techs can out-earn entry-level software engineers.
- Plumbers with their own businesses can make seven figures.

This industry has real financial opportunity, but we suck at communicating that.

We need to show young people, parents, teachers, and career counselors that this work is valuable, profitable, and full of growth opportunities.

STEP 3: BUILD A WORKFORCE THAT REFLECTS REALITY

Remember Sarah from earlier in the book? Let's check back in on her.

Sarah didn't just accept diversity; she built a company where different perspectives made the business better.

Here's her team:

- Marcus, her office manager, is in a wheelchair. He improved job scheduling efficiency by 30% with his logistics background.
- Javier, the child of an immigrant and her lead plumber, started as an apprentice and is now planning to buy the business from her.
- Jana, her sister, went from "just a secretary" to designing entire plumbing systems as a mechanical engineer.
- Tom, her 62-year-old master plumber, continues to work despite MS, thanks to adapted tools and flexible scheduling.

- Alex, her shorter-statured technician, has a modified service truck that allows him to work independently.
- Darnell, an African American veteran, transitioned from military service and became her most reliable emergency responder.
- Sarah didn't build a diverse team for the sake of diversity. She built the best team possible, and it just happened to be diverse.

THE BOTTOM LINE: IF YOU IGNORE WORKFORCE CHALLENGES, YOU WILL LOSE

The businesses that solve the labor shortage problem now will be the ones still standing in 10 years.

If you:

Build training programs

Partner with schools

Modernize your company culture

Embrace a wider talent pool

And show that the trades are lucrative, respected careers...

You won't just survive, you'll thrive.

THINKING PROMPT: ARE YOU READY TO BUILD THE FUTURE?

1. What are you currently doing to attract and retain employees?
2. Are you actively training your workforce, or just hoping good workers apply?
3. What partnerships could you create with local schools or trade programs?
4. Are you open to hiring a more diverse workforce, or are you limiting your options?

5. What's one immediate step you can take to strengthen your workforce strategy?

FINAL THOUGHT: THE FUTURE OF CONSTRUCTION DEPENDS ON YOU

If we don't invest in workforce solutions now, we won't have a workforce later.

It's that simple.

So, the question is:

Are you building a business for today? Or one that can survive the next decade?

The choice is yours.

CHAPTER 12
"I DON'T NEED A CRM"

AND OTHER LIES JACK TOLD HIMSELF

LINK, JACK, AND THE ART OF KEEPING CUSTOMERS FOR LIFE

For decades, Link built his HVAC business on relationships. He wasn't just the AC guy; he was the guy who remembered your mom was in the hospital, asked how your grand baby was sleeping, and showed up with a slice of Connie's famous apple cake when you'd had a rough week. He fixed systems, sure, but he also made people feel seen.

People didn't just call Link for repairs; they called because they trusted *him*.

But after the stroke, when he could no longer do the work, the phone didn't stop ringing. It rang for weeks. Then months. And even now, years later, it still rings from time to time.

Each time, he had to pick it up and say the words no small-town service provider ever wants to say: *"I'm sorry. I can't help."*

The relationships were real. The loyalty was earned. But when everything lived in his head, there was nothing left to pass on, except a phone that wouldn't stop ringing.

Link's story was one of legacy ... but not leverage. Jack's?

Jack was still in the thick of it. Running from job to job, trying to remember who needed what, when, and where.

He had great relationships too ... customers who liked him, trusted him ... but none of it was organized, repeatable, or scalable.

And unlike Link, Jack wasn't forced to stop... yet. But he was burning out fast.

That's when the intervention happened.

STEP 1: STOP RUNNING AROUND LIKE A MADMAN – THE SCHEDULING FIX

Jack's wife, Suzanne, and his longtime friend in the trades, yes, *that* Sarah ... staged a business intervention.

"Jack," Suzanne said, not even looking up from her coffee, "either get your business together or retire. You're working 70-hour weeks and making less than your nephew who bags groceries part-time."

Jack muttered something about needing a better calendar, but even he knew that wasn't the answer anymore.

Later that week, Sarah caught him at the supply house.

"Jack," she said, "you're drowning. Come by the office. I'll show you how we keep things running without losing our minds... or our profit margin."

Jack grumbled again. "I don't need some big corporate system. I just need my guys to show up and the checks to clear."

Sarah raised an eyebrow. "And yet here you are, forgetting appointments and doing paperwork at midnight. You coming by or not?"

He came by.

STEP 2: SCHEDULING THAT DIDN'T SUCK

Sarah started with his most obvious pain point: scheduling.

Before Sarah's help:

Jack scribbled appointments on scraps of paper and old receipts.

He forgot at least one job a month and rescheduled a dozen more. His crew often showed up late or unprepared because no one had clear info.

There were no reminders, no follow-ups, and definitely no rebookings.

After Sarah walked him through her setup:

Every job went into a system that tracked who, what, when, and where.

Crew schedules were visible, coordinated, and accurate.

Automated reminders kept customers in the loop.

Jack stopped carrying a clipboard and started carrying a coffee.

Within two weeks?

No more fire drills.

No more angry voicemails.

No more guessing.

Jack even caught himself whistling between jobs, because, for once, he wasn't behind.

STEP 3: FINALLY KEEPING TRACK OF CUSTOMERS (WITHOUT RELYING ON MEMORY ALONE)

Jack's biggest strength had always been his relationships. He had a sixth sense for who was worth working with, who was a pain, and who just needed a little nudge to say yes. He knew:

- Which general contractor always paid late

- Which property manager demanded discounts despite a million-dollar budget
- Who was "thinking about upgrading" but had been thinking about it for two years

Problem was, all of that lived in Jack's head.

So Sarah walked him through her tech stack, the systems she'd used to turn her father's chaotic plumbing business into a data-driven machine. She showed Jack how a CRM (Customer Relationship Management system) could take everything floating around in his brain and turn it into searchable, organized, team-accessible information.

She used one that integrated seamlessly with her other tools, scheduling, email, estimates, and accounting tools. It just so happened to be HubSpot, but the key was this: the system fit her business like a glove.

For Jack, that changed everything.

When a customer called, he could pull up their service history in seconds! On his phone!

His crew could see job notes and past issues, so they stopped walking in blind.

If a client mentioned a future panel upgrade, it got noted, and the system reminded him to follow up at the right time.

Within three months, Jack's revenue jumped. Not because he worked harder, because he stopped forgetting the low-hanging fruit.

STEP 4: INVOICING THAT DIDN'T MAKE HIM WANT TO SCREAM

Jack's old invoicing system was barely a system:

- Handwrite an invoice (if he remembered)
- Forget to send it for a week, or three

- Realize he undercharged because he forgot to include parts
- Chase the customer for payment... only to hear they "never got the invoice"

Sarah showed him how she linked her CRM to her accounting system (she used QuickBooks), so the process wasn't just easier—it was automated.

- Invoices were generated as soon as the job was marked complete.
- Late payment reminders went out automatically, without Jack playing bill collector.
- Payments could be collected online, no more waiting for a check in the mail.

Jack didn't just get paid faster. He got peace of mind. And for the first time in a long time, he wasn't leaving money on the table.

STEP 5: TRAINING THE TEAM TO USE THE SYSTEM (WITHOUT MUTINY)

Jack was sold. But his crew? Not so much.

His lead tech, Sam, grumbled: "So now I gotta be a secretary too?"

Jack just smirked. "Nope. You just have to stop writing notes on your hand and use the app."

To get buy-in, Jack:

- Tied performance bonuses to proper documentation
- Made sure every tech had mobile access to the system
- Automated reports so the crew could *see* their productivity improve

Within six months, even Sam came around. "Alright," he muttered one morning, "this actually makes life easier."

THE FINAL RESULT: A BUSINESS THAT DIDN'T NEED JACK TO FUNCTION

With better scheduling, customer tracking, invoicing, and follow-ups, Jack finally had a business that didn't fall apart without him.

Then one day, a larger electrical company from the next town over came knocking. They wanted to expand. They wanted Jack's book of business, his systems, and his steady revenue stream.

And for the first time, Jack realized something: His business was actually worth something.

He had a clean, organized customer database;

His revenue was predictable.

His crew could function without him.

They made an offer. Jack took it.

He didn't have to shut down. He didn't have to fade away. He walked away with a sale and with pride.

Jack Now? Mountain Life.

Jack occasionally helps the new owner troubleshoot the tricky jobs, but mostly? He's enjoying coffee on the porch of his mountain cabin.

No more lost invoices. No more 70-hour weeks. No more forgetting who needed what.

Jack built something that could outlive him as an owner. That's the real win.

FINAL THOUGHTS: SYSTEMS WORK, NO MATTER THE TRADE

Jack's story is about electrical work. But the same principles apply to every trade.

Whether you're in HVAC, plumbing, drywall, grading, or full-scale construction, getting your customer relationships, sched-uling, and follow-ups under control will:

- Increase revenue
- Reduce stress
- Build long-term value

The tools don't matter as much as the mindset. Start treating your business like it's worth something, because it is.

CHAPTER 13
A STRATEGIC PLAN
FOR A DIFFERENT FUTURE
THE BUSINESS THAT COULD HAVE BEEN

If I could rewrite history, I probably wouldn't change my father's business strategy. I just want him back, healthy and whole. I miss him terribly. Losing him gutted me.

So:

I'd erase the stroke.

I'd erase the slow, merciless unraveling of his mind.

I'd give him more years, healthy, happy, working if he wanted to.

But I don't have that power.

What I do have is a story, one that might finally drive home what so many business owners refuse to accept:

Tomorrow is not promised.

And if you wait too long to build a business that can outlive you, you'll leave behind nothing but phone calls your loved ones have to answer, explaining you're not coming back.

THE GAP BETWEEN GOALS AND REALITY

Small business owners love to set goals. They dream about growth, about "one day" getting things in order. But hope is not a strategy.

Most business owners don't fail because they aren't good at their trade.

They fail because they don't plan beyond the next job, the next quarter, the next payroll.

They say they'll get around to it.

Then one day, time runs out.

THE ALTERNATIVE UNIVERSE – WHAT IF LINK HAD A PLAN?

Let's rewind the clock.

What if, 10 years into running his business, my dad had approached it differently?

He was already great at what he did; his customers loved him. He had a full book of business.

But what if he had built a business that could stand on its own?

Go with me, let's pretend for a moment.

1995 – THE TURNING POINT

Picture Link sitting at the kitchen table, his worn notebook full of customer names, his invoices scattered in a mess only he understood. His business was making good money, but something gnawed at him.

"There's got to be more to this than just getting by."

He had two choices.

Option A: Keep doing what he was doing, show up, work hard, survive the slow seasons, and hope nothing happened to him.

Option B: Build a business that worked even when he wasn't holding it together by sheer willpower.

In this version of events, Link chose Option B.

THE FIRST STEPS – LAYING THE FOUNDATION

1. He Got Serious About Documentation.

Instead of relying on memory and scraps of paper, he:

- Created customer profiles with system details and service history.
- Wrote down his processes so someone else could follow them.
- Started tracking where money came in and where it leaked out.

2. He Hired and Trained Two Technicians.

Instead of working alone until his body gave out, he trained others. He started small, just two guys to take the overflow. This freed him up to focus on growing the business instead of just running service calls.

3. He Set Measurable Goals.

No vague dreams. Real numbers. Real deadlines.

Increase revenue by 20% next year.

Get 25% of customers on maintenance contracts.

Expand to a neighboring county in three years.

THE YEAR EVERYTHING CHANGED – 1998

This was the big one.

The maintenance contract program.

Link realized most of his customers didn't think about their HVAC systems until they broke.

So, he called them first.

He built a simple, predictable revenue stream.

25% of his clients signed up that first year.

That number doubled in five years.

Now, he wasn't just waiting for business; he had recurring revenue.

And for the first time ever, he had money coming in during the slow season.

THE POWER OF DATA - 2005

By now, Link had 900 clients.

And he knew everything about them.

Instead of running his business on gut instinct, he used data.

He tracked which systems were aging and reached out before they failed.

He ran targeted marketing based on past repairs.

He used a CRM system so every tech could pull up client history instantly.

By 2005, his business had crossed $3.5 million in annual revenue.

THE EXIT PLAN - 2010

At 60 years old, Link started thinking about what came next.

His business was now a machine.

20 employees.

A dedicated sales team.

Recurring revenue covering half his operating costs.

A business worth $4.7 million.

But there was one more critical piece.

THE REAL ENDGAME – WHO TAKES OVER?

Like many business owners, Link hoped a family member would step in.

But life had other plans.

So Link thought bigger.

THE EMPLOYEE BUYOUT PLAN

Instead of scrambling for a last-minute buyer, Link:

Created an Employee Stock Ownership Plan (ESOP).

Sold shares of the business over time to his team.

Guaranteed income for Link and his wife Connie, even after he stepped away.

By 2018, when the real Link suffered his stroke, this version of him?

He had already retired.

His business kept running without him.

And Connie? She wasn't fielding desperate calls from customers who still needed his help.

She was cashing checks from the company he built to outlive him.

THE REALITY CHECK – WHICH LINK ARE YOU?

This story is fictional. It hurt like hell to write it.

But the lesson is real.

Somewhere out there, a business owner just like my dad is still saying:

"I'll get to it later."

"My customers love me. They won't go anywhere."

"I just need to get through this season first."

Until one day, they can't work anymore.

And their life's work vanishes overnight.

YOUR ALTERNATIVE UNIVERSE STARTS TODAY

I can't rewrite history.

But you hold the pen to your future.

Ask yourself:

- If you were gone tomorrow, what would happen to your business?
- Does your revenue depend 100% on you showing up?
- Would someone actually want to buy your business, or does it disappear without you?

You can fix this.

But you have to start now.

Don't let your story end like the real Link's did.

Start building your legacy today.

CHAPTER 14
THE SUCCESS PATTERN
WHY SOME PEOPLE EXPAND & OTHERS SHRINK

THE REAL DIFFERENCE BETWEEN GROWTH AND STAGNATION

Success often seems like a mystery. Why do some people rise effortlessly while others struggle, despite working just as hard? After years of working with business owners, I've noticed a pattern. It's not luck. It's not talent. It's a specific way of thinking, deciding, and acting that makes all the difference.

To illustrate, let's talk about two contractors, Joe and Mike. Both started their businesses in the same year. Both had incredible skills. But ten years later, Joe was running a thriving, expanding business with a strong team and financial stability. Meanwhile, Mike was barely keeping the lights on, exhausted from working 14-hour days with nothing to show for it.

What was the difference? It wasn't work ethic. It wasn't intelligence. It was the way they approached growth, risk, and belief in themselves.

THE POWER OF BELIEF: WHAT YOU SEE IS WHAT YOU GET

In the world of advertising, you see this same principle at play. Companies don't invest millions into campaigns without believing in their impact. Take Liberty Mutual's *LiMu Emu*, a talking emu sidekick for an insurance commercial? On paper, it sounds ridiculous. But the creative team *believed* in the concept enough to make it work. Allstate's *Mayhem* campaign took a different approach, humorous but relatable. Both campaigns succeeded, but only because the teams behind them committed fully to their vision.

This is what separates those who expand from those who stay stuck: The ability to see possibility where others see risk. The confidence to commit to an idea without second-guessing.

The willingness to take strategic action, even when there's uncertainty.

THE SCIENCE OF PERCEPTION: HOW YOUR BRAIN SHAPES YOUR REALITY (YES, REALLY)

Your beliefs shape your opportunities. Science backs this up in two key ways:

1. The Observer Effect (Quantum Physics in Plain English)

In quantum physics, scientists discovered that the mere act of observing particles changes their behavior. What does that mean for you? It's a powerful metaphor for how our expectations influence outcomes. When you expect success, your actions shift, subtly but powerfully, toward making it real.

2. The Reticular Activating System (RAS): Your Brain's Search Engine

Ever notice how, when you decide to buy a new car, you suddenly see that model everywhere? That's your Reticular Activating System (RAS) at work. It filters information, prioritizing what's relevant. When you train your brain to look for success, opportunities that were always there become visible.

UNDERSTANDING YOUR WORTH: SUCCESS DOESN'T DEFINE YOU

No matter what you believe about our existence, whether you are Christian, a child of Mother Earth, or unaffiliated, it seems we've been conditioned to be productive little worker bees. If we aren't constantly grinding, the world tells us we are worthless slobs. But here's the truth: Productivity does not define your worth, and success, thus far, does not dictate what you deserve.

There is merit in quality work that improves the lives of others, absolutely. But there is far less merit in working ourselves to death under the illusion that we must earn the right to rest or the right to abundance. You deserve opportunities. You deserve success. Unless you suck, and that's just a whole different book.

TRAITS OF PEOPLE WHO EXPAND VS. PEOPLE WHO SHRINK

After working with countless entrepreneurs, I've identified the core traits that set apart those who expand from those who struggle:

The Expanders:

- They expect success. They don't just *hope* things work out; they operate as if they already have.
- They work strategically, not just hard. They avoid unnecessary struggle by focusing on high-impact actions.
- They believe in abundance. They see money, opportunities, and resources as available and flowing.

They align with what they do. They recognize when fear or hesitation is blocking their growth and take steps to overcome it. Like Ronda, a talented cosmetologist who struggled to rent chairs in her salon because she was apprehensive about managing people. Once she worked with a mentor, learned how to interview, and set expectations, she quickly had a waitlist for space in her salon.

The Shrinkers:

- They have a scarcity mindset. They make decisions from fear, hoarding resources, undercharging, or resisting investment.
- They equate success with struggle. They subconsciously believe that it's not "real" work if it's not hard.
- They fear outpacing others. Success feels dangerous; what if it alienates them? What if they're judged?
- They resist learning what they don't know. When faced with an unfamiliar aspect of their business, they avoid growth instead of seeking guidance. If Ronda hadn't found a mentor to help her navigate managing a team, she likely would have moved to a smaller space and worked alone. Instead, she now makes money even when she takes a day off.

THE POWER TO SHAPE YOUR REALITY

We have lived our lives with echoes of this message barely within earshot, just out of reach, never quite loud enough to absorb. And yet, there are a million sayings that hint at the truth: The ability to change our reality is within us, and it's far more powerful than we've been taught.

As Henry Ford said, *"Whether you think you can, or you think you can't, you're right."* The world has been whispering this message forever, but we've been conditioned to doubt it. Another reminder? *"You reap what you sow."* Your energy, your mindset, and your actions determine your outcome.

In fact, it's probably safe to say we weren't even taught the opposite; we were just never given the full picture. But here's what you need to know: Your power to shape your world in your favor is a universal truth, as real as sweet tea is delicious.

HOW TO SHIFT FROM STAGNATION TO GROWTH

If you recognize yourself in the 'shrink' category, don't worry. Change is possible, and it starts with awareness. Here's how:

1. Audit Your Beliefs – Take a sheet of paper and divide it into two columns. On one side, write down everything you believe about success, money, and growth. On the other side, challenge any statements that sound limiting. Ask yourself: 'Is this universally true, or is it just a belief I've picked up over time?' If it's limiting, rewrite it into a more empowering belief that supports expansion.

For example:

"Making money is always hard." → *"Making money can be easy when I focus on high-value work and smart strategies."*

"I'm not good at managing people." → *"I can become a great leader by learning and practicing new skills."*

2. Rewire Your Expectations – Every morning, affirm: "Why *not* me? I am fully capable of attracting new opportunities and success". Take the limitations away and watch how you talk about your prospects and your wins.

3. Take Strategic Action – Work *on* your business, not just *in* it. Plan, delegate, and invest in systems that create growth.

4. Surround Yourself with Expanders – If the people around you are constantly negative and you catch yourself on their bandwagon, get off! Limit your time with them and call them out when

necessary. Can't never could, right? Seek out those who think bigger and challenge you to grow.

The difference between expansion and stagnation isn't magic; it's a pattern. A predictable set of beliefs and actions that determine outcomes. The real question isn't *can* you grow, it's *Are you willing to step into that growth right now?*

I've been lucky enough to have expanders in my corner, people who believed in me when I was still finding my footing. One of the most influential was Ben Harrison.

Ben and I have known each other since the seventh grade, and when I started my agency, he became my very first client. But he wasn't just someone who hired me; he was someone who *truly valued my talent.* He believed in the power of what I was building long before I had a portfolio or polished pitch. He read what I wrote and said, "Yes. This helps people." He cheered me on when I was exhausted and doubting myself. He even paid for me to incorporate my business, to help validate what I had to offer.

Ben is a successful real estate broker with the rare ability to win at business while staying upbeat and gracious. His belief in me, and the doors he helped open, are a big reason why I get to write this book today. He's not just a friend. He's an embodiment of this success pattern I'm describing. Strategic. Supportive. Expansive.

So if you want to grow, surround yourself with people like Ben. Or better yet, *become* someone else's Ben.

Joe and Mike had the same starting point. The same skill. The same potential. But only one made the decision to expand instead of shrink. Only one took the leap, even when it felt uncomfortable. Only one built a thriving business.

Now, it's your turn. The path is in front of you. The tools are in your hands. Will you take the first step?

CHAPTER 15

THE MINDSET THAT BUILDS LEGACIES
(AND THE ONE THAT TEARS THEM DOWN)

I wish mindset didn't matter.

I wish hard work alone were enough. That effort, sweat, and sheer determination could guarantee success.

If that were true, my dad's business would have outlived him.

But it doesn't work that way. Hard work builds the business, but mindset determines if it survives.

And the worst part? You don't even see the damage until it's too late.

You can be the hardest-working person in the room and still run yourself into the ground.

You can pour everything into your business and still leave your family with nothing.

You can sabotage your success without ever realizing it.

Mindset is the quiet killer of small businesses.

And it has nothing to do with health, age, or luck.

So if you're stuck in hesitation, comfort, or flat-out denial, buckle up.

This chapter is might hurt a little ... but, it's also wrapped in encouragement.

A ROW HOUSE BY A CREEK: THE LESSONS THAT BUILT A MAN

My dad grew up in a little row house in Asco, West Virginia, right by the creek.

There was no indoor plumbing. Certainly, no HVAC.

Heat came from a wood stove, and in the bitter Appalachian winters, he and his brothers slept three to a bed, huddled under thick, homemade quilts to stay warm.

Dinner was pinto beans and cornbread because that's what they had. Meat wasn't just a treat; it was a luxury, and most nights, it wasn't on the table.

Dad never sugarcoated that part of his childhood.

He knew what poverty looked like.

More importantly, he knew what it *felt* like.

That kind of hunger stays with you. It teaches you to stretch a dollar. It makes you cautious with money. It teaches you that survival requires effort, every single day.

But he also saw those years as a kind of training.

A mindset bootcamp.

Because when you grow up with nothing, *everything* is earned.

Flora, my grandmother, raised nine kids after my grandfather passed, armed with grit, biscuits, and a fierce unwillingness to quit.

She got a job in a school kitchen, worked her way up, and eventually ran the place.

She didn't complain.

She didn't make excuses.

She just kept moving forward.

And that mindset didn't just shape my dad, it shaped *every single one* of Flora's kids:

- My Uncles, Roger and Darwin, ended up working for National Geographic. Roger's name is in the credits of older documentaries.

- My Aunt Lula went back to college as an adult and traced our family ancestry back centuries.
- My Aunt Eleanor ran the accounting department at a specialty printer.
- My Uncle Billy was a talented welder and fabricator.
- My Uncle Buddy worked as a prison guard, in fact, there is YouTube video of him giving a tour of one of the prisons he worked at.
- My Aunt Darlene was a devoted wife and wonderful mother.

Because when you are raised by a woman who refuses to quit, quitting doesn't even cross your mind.

Dad never quit either. But here's the truth: a lot of business owners, especially those raised like my dad, don't talk about:

GRIT CAN BUILD YOU, BUT IT CAN ALSO BLIND YOU

Mindset issues aren't always about giving up.

Sometimes they look like grinding harder than you need to.

Sometimes they sound like, *"This is just how we do it."*

And sometimes, they're the very reason you stay stuck ... not the economy, not your team, not your clients. You.

My dad carried the weight of that mindset, one shaped by necessity, forged in scarcity, and built for survival.

But survival and *scaling* are not the same thing.

What got him through childhood wasn't what could carry him through entrepreneurship.

And he wasn't alone in that.

MINDSET SHIFT #1: HARD WORK ALONE WON'T SAVE YOU

Dad was a worker. That's what he knew.

He worked harder than anyone I've ever seen.

But working hard and working smart are not the same thing.

And that's where a lot of business owners go wrong.

They build businesses that depend entirely on their own hands, their own brains, their own energy.

And then one day, they can't keep up.

Maybe it's an injury. Maybe it's burnout. Maybe it's just age.

And because they never documented, hired, trained, or built something that could run without them, the business dies the second they stop.

Hard work is a strength.

But if you don't combine it with strategy, it's also a trap.

The fix?

Start treating your business like it's bigger than you.

Build systems so your business runs even when you're not there.

Stop working yourself to death and start leading.

MINDSET SHIFT #2: FEAR IS THE BUSINESS KILLER YOU DON'T SEE COMING

You know what Dad wasn't afraid of?

- Heights
- Confined spaces
- 18-hour days in a crawl space full of cobwebs and God-knows-what

You know what did scare him?

Things he didn't fully understand.

- Business Technology
- Risk
- Sales

And guess what? That's exactly what kills most small businesses.

Fear of things you don't understand keeps you from:

Raising prices because "what if they say no?"

Hiring a second-in-command because "no one does it as well as I do."

Investing in marketing because "what if it doesn't work?"

Upgrading your systems because "I don't trust automation."

You think you're making safe decisions.

But safety isn't safety if it's keeping you small.

Fear doesn't mean stop.

Fear means pay attention.

Fear means whatever you are afraid of is probably EXACTLY the thing you need to do next.

MINDSET SHIFT #3: GET OUT OF YOUR OWN WAY

If you're stuck, overwhelmed, or working harder than ever with no progress, I'll bet good money the problem isn't your business.

It's you.

You probably already KNOW what you need to do.

So why aren't you doing it?

Perfectionism? ("*I need it to be just right before I launch.*")

Control issues? ("*No one can do it as well as me.*")

Fear of failure? ("*What if I mess this up?*")

Fear of success? ("*What if this actually works and I can't handle it?*")

If you want to grow, you HAVE to:

Delegate before you feel ready.

Raise prices before you think you deserve to.

Hire before you think you can afford it.

Implement systems before the chaos forces you to.

Your business will not grow beyond your own mindset. Period.

THE FINAL MINDSET SHIFT: LEGACY THINKING

Let's fast-forward. Imagine your own funeral.

(*Yes, I know that's dark, bear with me.*)

Your tools are put away.

Your truck is parked for the last time.

Your phone isn't ringing anymore.

And the people you leave behind?

They're not talking about your spreadsheets or how many jobs you closed.

They're not talking about the three weeks you spent debating a new work truck.

They're not talking about the nights you laid awake, panicked about your tax bill.

No.

They're talking about the crew you built and the families you helped feed.

They're talking about the high school scholarship you funded, the one that changed a kid's future.

They're talking about how you showed up, how you gave a damn, how you made an impact.

That's your legacy.

The clock's already running.

The only question is, what are you going to do about it?

You don't know how much time you have.

Neither did Dad.

Neither do I.

Neither do you.

But right now, you still have a choice.

So, stop running your business like you have forever.

CHAPTER 16
THE EXIT PLAN
YOU'LL WISH YOU HAD
EXIT STRATEGY & SUCCESSION PLANNING

Let's play a game called What Happens If You Disappear?

You wake up tomorrow and decide, "I'm done." Maybe you hit the lottery. Maybe you want to sail around the world. Maybe you've just had one too many run-ins with that one client who thinks HGTV makes them a construction expert.

What happens next?

- Do your employees know what to do without you, or will they be standing around like lost puppies?
- Can someone else run the business without it burning to the ground?
- Is there a plan for who takes over, or does your company become a chaotic free-for-all like a Black Friday sale at Walmart?
- Can you sell it for real money, or is this just an over-glorified job you've built for yourself?

If your answer is, "Oh crap, I have no idea," congratulations, you're in the majority.

MOST BUSINESS OWNERS HAVE NO EXIT PLAN

They assume they'll sell when they're ready. Or that their kids will gladly take over. Or that one day, they'll just retire and ride off into the sunset, drink in hand.

Spoiler alert: That's not how it works.

If you don't plan your exit, your business will make the decision for you, probably in the most inconvenient, expensive, and stress-inducing way possible. Let's make sure that doesn't happen.

WHY YOU NEED AN EXIT PLAN (EVEN IF YOU'RE NOT READY TO LEAVE)

Exit planning isn't just about selling your business. It's about creating options.

- You can sell for top dollar when the time comes (instead of scrambling for a buyer while stress-eating Tums).
- You can step back without everything falling apart (because a real business isn't a one-man circus).
- Your family isn't left untangling a dumpster fire if something happens to you.
- You have control over who takes over, so your legacy doesn't end up in the hands of your clueless cousin who thinks Excel is a workout plan.

Every business will eventually change hands or cease to exist, either voluntarily or involuntarily. Smart owners prepare before they're forced to.

If you've built something worth keeping, protect it. If you want to cash out, position yourself to actually get paid. And if your plan is to work until you keel over on a job site, well... at least have a will, because your family shouldn't have to deal with that mess.

The bottom line? If you don't take charge of your exit, your exit will take charge of you. And trust me, that's never the fun way to go.

THE 4 MAIN EXIT OPTIONS

There are only a few ways to leave your business. Let's break them down:

1. Selling to a Third Party

This is the dream scenario, you cash out, walk away, and someone else takes over. But selling isn't as easy as slapping a "For Sale" sign on the door. You need:

- A Profitable, Documented Business – Buyers want systems, not chaos.
- Consistent Revenue & Contracts – Predictable income makes your business attractive.
- A Strong Brand & Marketing Engine – A business that can run without you.
- Clean Financials – No one buys a mess.

If you ever want to sell, start making your business buyer-friendly NOW.

2. Family Succession (Handing It Down to Your Kids)

This is where a lot of small business owners assume their story will go.

"My son/daughter will take over one day."

Will they? Have you asked them?

Many kids don't want the business, at least, not without structure. If you plan to pass it down:

- Start training them years before you step away.
- Put the business in writing (not just family assumptions).
- Have a clear leadership transition to avoid resentment.
- Make sure they want it, not just feel obligated.

Otherwise, you might leave them a burden, not a legacy.

3. Employee or Management Buyout (ESOPs & MBOs)
Your best buyer might already work for you.
Many businesses transition to longtime employees through:

- ESOP (Employee Stock Ownership Plan) – Employees buy shares over time.
- Management Buyout – Key employees purchase the business directly.

This works when you have great leadership in place. If you want to go this route:

- Identify potential buyers early
- Train them in business operations (not just technical work)
- Create a structured buyout plan over several years

Done right, this keeps the business stable and thriving, even after you leave.

. . .

4. Closing the Doors (The Worst-Case Scenario)

If you don't plan your exit, this is what happens:

Your family is stuck figuring out what to do.

Employees lose their jobs overnight.

Your business value drops to zero.

Without an exit plan, this is where you're headed.

HOW JACK SOLD HIS BUSINESS FOR MORE THAN HE EXPECTED

Jack had always planned to sell his electrical business. He figured after decades of wiring up homes, fixing circuit breakers, and handling the town's emergency calls, he could get around $500,000 for the company, mostly based on assets, goodwill, and a solid reputation.

Then he discovered maintenance contracts.

One day, a local private school, St. Matthew's Academy, asked Jack if there was a way to save money on service calls. Their aging building had constant electrical issues, and they were paying through the nose every time something failed.

Jack had never considered selling maintenance contracts before. But he asked his HVAC buddy Ted, who ran a successful company, and Ted laughed:

"Jack, you already *do* maintenance, you're just not charging for it ... probably at all, let alone ahead of time. You're tightening panels and checking breakers every time you step foot in a building. Package that, bill it annually, and now it's a service."

Jack started researching. He checked with his supply house, found an industry seminar on electrical maintenance plans, and started running some numbers.

Then Jack looked at North Central Plastics, a small manufacturer in town renting an older building. They were paying nearly $35,000 a year in emergency calls, just to keep their production line from falling apart.

So Jack pitched something new:

A $1,500/month maintenance contract.

That's $18,000 a year, *less* than what they were already spending.

But they hesitated.

"$18K upfront? For what exactly?"

Jack hesitated too. He wasn't used to billing *before* problems happened.

It felt backward. Risky. What if they said no?

But he walked them through it:

- 30% reduction in emergency calls.
- Priority response: no more waiting when things broke.
- Predictable costs instead of surprise repair bills
- Documentation of all inspections and maintenance tasks.
- No scope creep: because this covered *maintenance,* not new installs, system upgrades, or major parts.

They said yes.

Six months in, North Central saw fewer breakdowns and more uptime. But that wasn't the real story.

Because that $18,000?

It turned into $145,000 that year.

Why?

Because once Jack got regular access to the site, he spotted major inefficiencies and safety issues.

- He upgraded their outdated system (billable).
- Repaired faulty panels (also billable).
- Replaced parts that were well outside the scope of the maintenance plan (definitely billable).

The maintenance plan opened the door.

The real revenue came from being in the building, building trust, and solving bigger problems.

HOW THIS AFFECTED JACK'S BUSINESS SALE

Jack's business went from a good local shop to a predictable cash-flow machine. Buyers love predictable revenue.

Instead of selling for $500,000, Jack got $1.2 million, because the business wasn't just based on his labor anymore.

FINAL THOUGHT: THE BUSINESS THAT OUTLIVES YOU

Your business is more than just a paycheck. It's your legacy.

If you build it right, it can provide for your family, your employees, and your community long after you're gone.

So the question isn't *if* you'll leave one day. The question is:

Will your business still be standing when you do?

If the answer isn't clear, start fixing it today.

CHAPTER 17
MONEY, THE BEST EMPLOYEE YOU'LL EVER HAVE
(IF YOU STOP TREATING IT LIKE TRASH)

Money is weird.

When you don't have it, you obsess over it. When you do have it, you either hoard it like a Depression-era squirrel or spend it like you just got drafted into the NFL.

Business owners, in particular, have a complicated relationship with money.

You start your company with dreams of making more than you did in that soul-sucking job. You tell yourself, *Once I'm running my own business, I'll finally be in control of my income! I'll pay myself more! I'll be rich!*

Fast-forward a few years, and suddenly you're the brokest "successful" person you know.

You're bringing in more revenue than ever, but somehow...you feel like you have less money. Your bank account fluctuates so wildly it gives you motion sickness. And worst of all?

Your business is making money. You just never seem to keep any of it.

WHAT I LEARNED THE HARD WAY (SO YOU DON'T HAVE TO)

I've run a service-based business for years. I never treated my company like an ATM. My books were clean. I wasn't making reckless financial decisions.

And yet, when my dad got sick, I had to step away for a while.

No sales were happening.

But payroll? Payroll was still rolling out as if we were still bringing in an extra $10K a month.

I was bleeding cash and didn't even realize it right away, because I was grieving. I wasn't looking at the numbers. I wasn't making adjustments.

I *could* get a loan, thankfully.

But if I'd had a bigger cash reserve? I might not have needed it. If I'd realized what was happening sooner? I could have adjusted earlier, even if it was as simple as making sure the team was running ads while I was away.

Business owners always assume the danger is in bad decisions.

But sometimes? The danger is in not deciding at all.

Ignoring your numbers doesn't make the problem go away.

And whether your crisis is grief, burnout, an economic downturn, or just a slow season, you cannot afford to be asleep at the wheel when it comes to your money.

REVENUE IS NOT PROFIT (SO STOP BRAGGING ABOUT IT)

You ever meet that guy who brags about his million-dollar business like he's rolling in cash?

Yeah, ask him how much he actually takes home.

Revenue is vanity. Profit is sanity. Positive cash flow, that is PEACE!

If you're bringing in $1 million a year but only keeping $75K, you don't have a million-dollar business. You have a low-paying, high-stress job.

The goal isn't just making money. It's keeping it.

THE "OH SH*T" FUND: WHY YOUR BUSINESS NEEDS A CASH CUSHION

Listen, something will go wrong.

Maybe your biggest client suddenly goes under. Maybe your truck engine dies. Maybe the IRS shows up like, *"Hey, remember us?"*

If you don't have cash reserves, every setback is a crisis.

And when you're in crisis mode, you make desperate decisions.

That's how you end up:

Taking out high-interest loans

Maxing out credit cards

Robbing Peter to pay Paul

The fix? Save like the bad times are already here.

A three-month cash reserve (meaning three months' worth of operating expenses in the bank) isn't a luxury; it's survival.

That money buys you time when life inevitably punches you in the gut.

YOUR BUSINESS IS NOT YOUR PERSONAL ATM

Somewhere along the way, a lot of business owners get confused about whose money is whose.

They treat their business bank account like a personal slush fund, pulling money whenever they "need" it, without paying attention to whether the business can afford it.

This is how you wake up one day realizing:

- You've drained the business dry and can't make payroll.
- You owe the IRS more than you have in the bank.
- You have no emergency cushion for slow months.
- You can't get a business loan because your finances are a dumpster fire.

Here's the truth: You need to pay yourself like a responsible adult, not a teenager with a cash-stuffed birthday card.

The Fix? Set yourself a real salary and stick to it. If the business can't afford to pay you regularly, your pricing or cash flow is broken.

IS YOUR BUSINESS BANKABLE? BECAUSE RIGHT NOW, IT'S PROBABLY NOT.

Want to know why so many small business owners can't get a loan when they need one?

Because their books look like they were written in crayon.

If you want banks and investors to take you seriously, your financials need to be:

1. Clean (No "mystery expenses" or cash disappearing into the void)
2. Consistent (Not just one good year followed by five bad ones)
3. Documented (Not just "it's in my head" or "I keep track in a notebook")

You know what's sexy to banks and buyers? A business that runs like a real company.

Get your financial house in order, because when opportunities come, you don't want to be the guy saying, *"Wait, let me clean up my QuickBooks first."*

FINAL THOUGHT: YOU'LL NEVER OUT-EARN A BAD FINANCIAL HABIT

A lot of business owners think, *"I just need to make more money."*

And yes, revenue growth is important.

But you can't out-earn poor financial discipline.

If you don't fix your spending, pricing, and financial habits now, it won't matter how much you make. You'll always feel broke.

WHAT TO DO NEXT (IF YOU WANT TO ACTUALLY KEEP YOUR MONEY)

1. Get Real About Your Numbers – If you don't know your profit margins, fix that today.
2. Stop Treating Your Business Like a Personal ATM – Pay yourself correctly, not chaotically.
3. Build a Cash Reserve – Stop living month to month.
4. Make Sure Your Business is Bankable – Keep clean financials so you can get funding when needed.
5. Work With an Accountant – No, your "buddy who's good at math" doesn't count.

Your business should make you money. It should give you freedom, security, and options.

If it's not doing that? You don't have a business. You have a job.

Fix your financial house now, so when opportunity knocks, you're ready to answer.

CHAPTER 18
STOP HIDING IN THE SHADOWS
MARKETING ISN'T OPTIONAL

Let's play a new game. We are having fun, okay!

Imagine for a second that marketing doesn't exist.

You don't have a website.

No logo. No business cards.

No Google listing.

No Facebook page where your aunt leaves embarrassing comments about how proud she is of you.

All you have is a van, some tools, and your skills.

So you drive around town hoping someone flags you down like a lost taxi in the 1940s. Maybe you stand in the grocery store yelling, *"Hey! Need a plumber? I fix toilets!"*

Or you leave handwritten notes on windshields, begging people to call you before the paint starts peeling off their shutters.

That sounds insane, right?

AND YET, this is exactly how most business owners approach marketing.

They exist but don't really show up.

They have a website, but it looks like it was built on Netscape in 1999.

They're on social media, but post once every six months when they remember they have a business page.

They rely on word-of-mouth, but never ask for reviews, referrals, or do anything to fuel that machine.

And then they wonder why they aren't growing.

Spoiler alert: If no one knows you exist, they can't hire you.

Which brings us to Sarah.

SARAH'S MARKETING TRANSFORMATION: FROM "WE'LL SEE" TO "LET'S SCALE"

Sarah's Precision Plumbing was already successful.

They had:

Trucks wrapped with their logo (mobile billboards, baby)

A simple website with their phone number

A reputation for great work

But Sarah wasn't satisfied with just "staying busy."

She wanted to build something bigger, a business that didn't just bring in jobs this month, but one that attracted customers consistently, even when she wasn't thinking about it.

So she stopped guessing and started marketing like she meant it.

Here's how:

STEP 1: TURNING THE WEBSITE FROM A BUSINESS CARD INTO A 24/7 SALES MACHINE

Sarah's website was fine. It had her number. A list of services. Maybe even a stock photo of a guy in a tool belt (who had probably never fixed a sink in his life).

But "fine" doesn't make money.

So Sarah leveled up:

1. Made online booking idiot-proof (one big, fat "Book Now" button).
2. Added a lead magnet, a free guide called *"10 Ways to Prevent a Plumbing Disaster"* in exchange for email addresses.
3. Built an FAQ section so customers could get answers before calling (reducing wasted time).
4. Started a blog with ACTUAL USEFUL INFO (*"Why is my toilet making a sound like a dying whale?"*).

The result?

Her website wasn't just sitting there anymore; it was working. Potential customers could:

- Find her on Google (thanks to keyword-rich blog posts).
- Book a job at 2 AM without having to talk to a human.
- Join her email list, so she could keep warming them up until they were ready to hire her.

STEP 2: CAPTURING AND NURTURING LEADS (SO THEY DON'T FORGET YOU EXIST)

Fun fact: 97% of people who visit a website leave without taking action.

Sarah wasn't about to let all those leads go to waste.

So she:

Captured their emails with that free guide.

Sent automated follow-ups, offering maintenance tips and small discounts to book a service.

Used remarketing ads, so her website visitors started seeing

Precision Plumbing ads EVERYWHERE (Facebook, Instagram, news sites, even in their dreams).

Soon, people started saying: *"It's like I was JUST thinking about calling a plumber, and then I saw your ad!"*

Yeah, Susan. That's the science of marketing.

STEP 3: GETTING CUSTOMERS TO DO THE MARKETING FOR HER

Sarah didn't stop once she got the job.

She knew that happy customers = more customers.

So she built a simple system:

1. After every job, customers got an automated email asking for a review (with a direct link, because no one likes hunting for the "Leave a Review" button).
2. She educated her customers about how leaving reviews helps small businesses thrive.
3. She personally thanked them because appreciation goes a long way.

The result?

More Google reviews = higher search rankings.

More referrals = lower marketing costs.

Her customers became her marketing team.

STEP 4: HIRING A MARKETING PRO (BECAUSE AIN'T NOBODY GOT TIME FOR THAT)

Sarah had systems in place. Her website was bringing in leads.

But she knew marketing was a full-time job.

So she stopped trying to do it all herself and hired help.

She brought in a marketing team that:

1. Ran her ads (so she wasn't just throwing money at Facebook and hoping for the best).
2. Tracked every dollar spent (so she knew exactly what was working).
3. Created content (so she wasn't scrambling to post on social media at the last minute).

And most importantly, they set up HubSpot so she could track every customer, every email, every quote, and every sale in one place.

Because here's the truth:

If you don't have time to market, hire someone who does.

If you don't know how marketing works, hire someone who does.

If your website was built in 2005 and still looks like it, FOR THE LOVE OF ALL THAT IS HOLY, fix it.

THE RESULTS: A BUSINESS THAT RUNS ITSELF (EVEN WHEN SHE'S ON VACATION)

Within one year of getting serious about marketing, Sarah saw:

40% more new customers.

25% more repeat business.

Fewer slow seasons.

Higher profits WITHOUT working longer hours.

And the best part?

Precision Plumbing became an ASSET, not just a job.

When she wanted to sell, her business was worth more because she had a real marketing system in place.

Buyers weren't just paying for her reputation; they were paying for a business that kept growing, without her.

LESSON: YOU CAN KEEP GUESSING, OR YOU CAN BUILD A MACHINE

Marketing isn't about being "flashy" or "salesy."

It's about making sure people who NEED you can FIND you.

You can hope for referrals, or you can create a system that generates them.

You can rely on word-of-mouth, or you can build a brand people recognize.

You can keep saying 'I should probably update my website,' or you can fix it and start making money.

Your business is either growing or dying.

Marketing is the missing link between where you are and where you want to be.

So the question is:

Are you ready to stop guessing?

CHAPTER 19
STAYING TOP OF MIND WITHOUT CHASING LEADS

Jack had been in the electrical business for decades, but marketing? That was another beast entirely.

For years, his strategy was what most service-based businesses do: do good work, get referrals, maybe throw up a yard sign here and there, and call it a day.

And to be fair, it worked. Until it didn't.

The problem wasn't that Jack wasn't getting customers. It's that he wasn't staying top of mind.

THE WAKE-UP CALL

Jack was at a Chamber of Commerce networking event, casually talking shop with a commercial property manager he'd worked with in the past.

"Hey, Jack," the guy said, taking a sip of his beer, "we just had a big electrical overhaul done at our north location last month. Could've used you on that one."

Jack blinked. Wait. What?

"Who'd you go with?" Jack asked, trying to keep his voice casual.

"Ahh, some newer company in town, saw their case study on LinkedIn and figured I'd give 'em a shot."

Jack's flabbers were ghasted!

He'd literally worked on that same company's flagship building a year ago. They knew him. They trusted him. But the reality was they forgot about him.

Because he wasn't showing up in their world.

And that's when it hit him: Doing great work isn't enough. You have to remind people you exist.

SHIFTING FROM "WORD OF MOUTH" TO "TOP OF MIND"

Jack wasn't about to start making TikTok videos dancing with electrical panels.

But he could start being more intentional about showing up in front of his ideal clients without feeling like he was "selling".

He sat down with his "web guy", a title Jack had been using for years, even though the man ran a full-service marketing firm, led a team of five, and had more certifications than Jack had extension cords.

Jack called him the "web guy", the same way people call me the "marketing girl" or "website gal", as if the entire scope of modern marketing could be reduced to clicking around in Canva and changing your business hours on Google.

The truth?

Marketing today is multi-disciplinary, multi-dimensional, and changing faster than a hummingbird on espresso can flap its tiny wings.

You need someone who understands copywriting, brand voice, automation, analytics, design, user behavior, SEO, PPC, CRM integration, and about 47 acronyms you've never heard of.

That's your "web guy."

Jack had ignored him for years.

But now, sitting across from him, bleary-eyed and borderline desperate, he finally asked the question that changed everything.

"Alright," Jack said, rubbing his temples, "How do I stay visible without annoying people?"

His web guy grinned. "Now you're asking the right question."

STEP ONE: TELL STORIES, NOT SALES PITCHES

People love stories. They remember them. They relate to them.

Jack's first move? Case studies.

Instead of bland "we do electrical work" posts, he started sharing before-and-after transformations from real clients.

A warehouse that saved thousands in energy costs after upgrading their old lighting system. A restaurant that finally stopped tripping breakers during dinner rush after a panel upgrade. A homeowner who avoided a near-disaster because Jack caught a major wiring issue during a routine inspection.

Each story ended with a soft call to action: "If you've got an older panel, now's the time to get it checked before peak season hits. Give us a call!"

The result? People saw Jack as the guy who solves problems, not just another electrician.

THE STORY BEHIND THE BUSINESS

But there was another layer Jack hadn't considered: the stories behind his business. The ones his customers never heard.

His early days learning the trade from his uncle. The time he took a risk and started the business out of his garage. The way his team grew from a one-man shop to a crew of five, all with their own journeys and strengths.

These weren't made-up marketing gimmicks. These were real, human, emotional connections that gave people a reason to care.

People don't just buy services, they buy into people. And when your audience knows your why, they're more likely to trust you, refer you, and remember you.

This is where Donald Miller's *Building a StoryBrand* hits the nail on the head. Your business isn't the hero. Your customer is. But your backstory, your values, your vision, they're what let the customer know they've found the right guide.

So Jack started weaving those stories in, too. Posts like:

- "Why I still carry my first set of lineman pliers in my tool bag."
- "The mistake that nearly made me quit, and why I'm glad I didn't."
- "Meet Trevor: From apprentice to foreman in 18 months."

These weren't just good stories. They were powerful positioning tools. And they made Jack more than just another contractor; they made him memorable.

STEP TWO: NOT ANOTHER NEWSLETTER

Jack used to think newsletters were spammy, inbox-clogging garbage.

And to be fair, *most of them are.*

You've seen 'em:

"We're running a special!"

"Here's a coupon you'll never use!"

"Check out this stock photo of "our team" pretending to laugh in a circle!"

Jack's reaction?

Hard pass.

He didn't want to send something that was as "useless as tits on a boar".

But then his "web guy" broke it down for him:

People don't hate newsletters.

They hate bad newsletters.

So Jack started sending stuff that actually mattered:

Checklist-style tips like "5 Things Every Business Should Check Before Storm Season"

Entertaining fails like "Don't Let This Be You: The Time Someone Tried to Fix a Panel with a Butter Knife"

Timely reminders like "When's the Last Time You Had a Load Test?"

Customers didn't just open them.

They replied.

They forwarded them to friends.

And most importantly, they remembered Jack when it counted.

STEP THREE: SOCIAL MEDIA WITHOUT THE BS

Jack's new approach to social media? Be human. Be helpful. Be present.

No sleazy sales tactics. Just showing up with useful info and personality.

Behind-the-scenes photos of his team on job sites. Quick home safety tips to prevent electrical fires. A running "fix of the week" post featuring ridiculous DIY fails (with a gentle "Call a pro next time" nudge). Shoutouts to clients: "Big thanks to XYZ Company for trusting us with their new build! Excited to see this project come to life."

Did everyone engage? Nope.

But when someone did need an electrician, guess who they remembered? Jack.

STEP FOUR: GETTING INVOLVED IN THE COMMUNITY

Jack also got out from behind his desk.

He started:
- Sponsoring a local Little League team.
- Speaking at business networking events.
- Partnering with an HVAC company for a cross-promoted safety webinar.

People started seeing his name everywhere. Not in an annoying way, but in a "Oh yeah, Jack's our guy" kind of way.

STEP FIVE: THE SUBTLE ART OF SELLING WITHOUT SELLING

Here's what Jack learned: You don't have to shove your services down people's throats. You just have to be the first person they think of when they need help.

By staying in their world, through stories, value, humor, and real engagement, Jack tripled his referral business.

The kicker? That commercial property manager who hired another company?

A year later, he called Jack for an even bigger job.

"Hey Jack," he said. "You know, I've been seeing all your posts about energy efficiency upgrades. We've got a few buildings that could use a second look. Think you can come by?"

Jack grinned. "Absolutely."

THE TAKEAWAY: YOUR BRAND IS A LIVING THING, FEED IT

Too many businesses treat marketing like an afterthought.

Jack learned that if you're not consistently showing up, you're making it easy for clients to forget you.

So if you're not actively staying top of mind, ask yourself:

When was the last time my clients heard from me, without me selling them something?

Do I have a way to share success stories and educate my audience?

Is my brand just a logo, or am I actually building relationships?

Are my values and origin stories part of my message, or just memories I keep to myself?

At the end of the day, marketing isn't about making noise, it's about making connections.

And when you get that part right? Your business doesn't just grow. It becomes unforgettable.

CHAPTER 20
WHEN THE WATERS RISE
BUSINESS CONTINUITY & DISASTER PLANNING

In the wake of Hurricane Helene, business owners across North Carolina were forced to answer a question they had likely never asked themselves before: *What if everything was gone tomorrow? Correction: everything IS gone ... TODAY!*

For some, the answer was heartbreaking. Entire businesses wiped out, equipment lost, offices flooded beyond repair. Some never reopened. Others fought tooth and nail to rebuild, realizing in hindsight just how unprepared they had been.

And then there were the lucky few, the ones who had *a plan.* The ones who had the right insurance coverage, detailed documentation of assets, backup systems in place, and, most importantly, the ability to pivot quickly when disaster struck.

These are the business owners who didn't just survive. They came back stronger.

THE HARD TRUTH: MOST BUSINESS OWNERS AREN'T PREPARED

"I can't tell you how many times I've sat across from a business owner after a disaster, and the first words out of their mouth are, 'I thought I was covered.'"

That's what Michelle O'Connor, owner of an independent insurance agency in North Carolina, shared when I asked her how businesses fared after the flooding.

"The truth is, a lot of business owners don't know what their policy actually covers. They assume 'business insurance' means 'everything's covered.' But things like flood damage? Business interruption? Equipment replacement? If you don't have specific policies in place, you're probably out of luck."

And it's not just massive natural disasters that can cripple a business. Fires, theft, cyberattacks, supplier disruptions, any of these can throw a business into chaos if there's no continuity plan in place.

The biggest mistake? Thinking 'It won't happen to me.'

"I get it," Michelle continued. *"No one wants to think about worst-case scenarios. But the difference between the businesses that bounced back and the ones that closed their doors? The ones who made it had planned ahead."*

THE REALITY OF REBUILDING: ZILLICOAH BREWING'S FIGHT TO SURVIVE

Sometimes, even when you prepare, disaster still takes everything.

That's what happened to Zillicoah Brewing, a craft brewery in Asheville, North Carolina, that was wiped out in the aftermath of Hurricane Helene.

They knew their location was in a floodplain, so they built

accordingly. They raised their electrical systems. They mounted their equipment higher than the 500-year flood mark. They thought they were ready.

Then, the water came.

Six feet of it.

Inside the building.

It wasn't a flood, it was a lake.

Owner John Parks recounted the devastation in an episode of *On the Blue Ridge*, a podcast featuring the most impactful voices in the Blue Ridge Mountains in the wake of this disaster. He described how he drove down as soon as the rain stopped, but he couldn't even reach the building.

"Tractor-trailers were floating by."

By the time the floodwaters receded three days later, what he found was absolute emptiness.

"We walked in, and there was nothing in there. Absolutely wiped out."

The north end of the building had collected debris, logs, furniture, parts of homes that had been ripped apart upstream. The south end? It looked like it had been stripped clean.

The river had taken everything.

And because they were in a flood zone, they couldn't get insurance.

"Everyone checks in on day three," Parks said in an earlier interview with the Asheville Citizen-Times. *"But it's month three when everyone really needs help."*

And yet, they're rebuilding.

They're fighting to bring Zillicoah back, even knowing they may never fully recover what they lost.

(*Information in this section was sourced from the Asheville Citizen-Times and podcast On the Blue Ridge, featuring John Parks.*)

COULD YOUR BUSINESS SURVIVE A DISASTER?

Zillicoah's story raises some critical questions:

- Are you financially prepared for the worst?
- Do you have the right coverage, or are you one disaster away from losing it all?
- If your physical location was wiped out, could you operate from somewhere else?
- Could your business survive three months with no revenue?

Because while you might not be in a flood zone, there are a thousand ways your business could face an unexpected crisis.

- A fire
- A cyberattack
- A personal emergency that takes you away from your work

The businesses that survive aren't always the biggest or the most successful.

They're the ones who planned ahead.

And if you haven't, there's no better time to start than right now.

STEP 1: KNOW WHAT YOU HAVE (AND WHAT IT'S WORTH)

Let's talk about documentation.

If disaster struck right now, your shop flooded, your truck was stolen, or a fire tore through your office, do you have a record of everything you own?

Not just what's in your QuickBooks account, but actual proof of assets?

- A current inventory of equipment, tools, and materials?
- Receipts or records of major purchases?
- Photos or videos documenting your workspace and inventory?
- Serial numbers for high-value items?

"The first thing adjusters ask after a disaster is, 'Can you prove what you lost?'" Michelle said. *"If you don't have documentation, you're relying on memory and a lot of goodwill. That's not a position you want to be in."*

Pro tip: Take 15 minutes to walk through your shop, job site, or office and take photos or a video of everything. Store it in the cloud where you can access it from anywhere.

STEP 2: DON'T JUST INSURE THE STUFF, INSURE THE BUSINESS

One of the biggest misconceptions business owners have? Thinking insurance is just about replacing damaged equipment.

It's not.

Sure, replacing tools, trucks, and office equipment is important. But what about the income you lose while you rebuild?

Imagine a small electrical company in western North Carolina. Their shop didn't flood, but their suppliers' warehouses did. Suddenly, materials were backordered for months, pushing project deadlines back indefinitely. No work meant no income.

What if you couldn't work for weeks, or even months?

That's where business interruption insurance comes in. It can help cover:

- Lost revenue while your business is shut down.
- Rent or mortgage payments while you can't operate.
- Payroll costs to keep your team afloat.
- Temporary relocation costs if you need to move operations.

And yet, Michelle shared, *"Most small business owners don't even realize this type of coverage exists until they desperately need it."*

STEP 3: HAVE A BACKUP PLAN (BEFORE YOU NEED ONE)

A solid business continuity plan isn't just about insurance. It's about knowing exactly how your business would function in a crisis.

Ask yourself:

- If your physical location were destroyed, where would you operate from?
- If your key suppliers went down, do you have backup vendors?
- If your team couldn't work on-site, could they work remotely?
- If your systems crashed, do you have backups of critical data?

Zillicoah Brewery, that small business in North Carolina that was devastated by flooding, is still fighting to recover.

Compare that to the Erwin, TN company that lost both workers and infrastructure in the same disaster. A tragedy on multiple levels, and a stark reminder that some losses aren't just financial, they're permanent.

A continuity plan doesn't guarantee survival. But not having one almost guarantees failure.

CHAPTER 21
THE OWNER'S ROLE IN GROWTH & SCALABILITY

In December of 2023, my world started to shift. My dad's health was declining fast, and my mom needed me. She needed all of us: my daughter and my youngest son. We took turns spending the night at their house because she was struggling, both emotionally and physically. Watching the strongest man I had ever known fade away was unbearable. But there was no time to process. He needed us. She needed us.

And my business? It needed me, too. But for the first time, I wasn't there.

I have an amazing team, and they carried on. They handled client work. They managed hard conversations with customers who didn't understand why I wasn't around. As if that wasn't obvious.

And when Dad left us in late March, I left too. My mom and I packed up and went to the coast for two weeks. We sat by the ocean, trying to understand how we were supposed to move forward without our True North.

And while we grieved, the business kept going, sort of.

WHAT I LEARNED WHEN I STEPPED AWAY

The first thing I realized? The company could function without me. That was a win. Operations didn't collapse. Projects got done. Clients were served.

But then came the hard truth: the business wasn't growing.

Mandy, my right-hand, one of my best friends, took sales calls when they came in. KJ, my soul sister and ride-or-die, wanted to step in more, but she was new to the team. She didn't yet know the right questions to ask.

Nobody was actively selling. Nobody was building relationships or uncovering new opportunities. And that was a problem.

Because sales, for better or worse, had always been me.

I don't even like sales, but I'm good at it. I don't push people, I listen. I understand what they need, and if I can help, I tell them. If I can't, I tell them that, too. It's natural for me. It's part of how I've built this business. But for those months? I wasn't making connections. I wasn't asking questions. I wasn't there.

WHAT HAPPENS WHEN THE GROWTH ENGINE STALLS

That stretch of time taught me something crucial:

My team is incredible and can handle operations.

My company has structure, systems, and sustainability.

But growth? That stops without a plan.

Because without new sales, the work pipeline dries up.

I was still making payroll like we had the best year ever. But we weren't. We were down $10K a month in revenue. And I wasn't there to course-correct.

I had the reserves to keep going. I was able to get a loan. But had I been paying attention, had I been more proactive about building a sales system that wasn't just ME, I might not have needed that loan at all.

BUILDING A BUSINESS THAT GROWS WITHOUT YOU

The biggest mistake business owners make is thinking that "scalability" just means more revenue, more staff, more systems.

But the reality is, scalability means:

You're not the only one selling.

Operations don't stall because you step away.

The business doesn't just run, it grows.

I built something strong, but I hadn't built it to grow without me.

And that had to change.

THE PLAN: REPLACING MYSELF IN SALES

It's not just about training someone to take sales calls. It's about systemizing what I do naturally.

- Clarifying our ideal clients. No more talking to just anyone. Who is the best fit? What industries? What problems do we solve best?
- Creating a process. Sales isn't magic. It's a repeatable conversation. What do I ask? What do I listen for? What makes someone say yes?
- Training the team. KJ wants to step up. So she will. She'll get the scripts, the confidence, the framework. She'll learn to sell like I do, but in her own way.
- Building a real sales engine. No more relying on "who happens to find us." We'll run ads. We'll generate inbound leads. We'll create a system that feeds itself.

THE LEGACY LINK: A BUSINESS THAT THRIVES BEYOND THE OWNER

This entire book is about building something that lasts. Something that isn't just a paycheck. Something that creates real, transferable value.

What I learned in the hardest year of my life is this: You don't know when you'll be forced to step away.

And if you haven't prepared for that moment? The business will suffer.

So now I ask you:

- If you disappeared for three months, would your business still grow?
- Have you trained someone else to do the things you do best?
- Are you running a business that scales or just a business that survives?

If you don't like your answers, fix it now.

Because your Legacy Link isn't just about what you build today; It's about what endures when you're gone.

CHAPTER 22
LEVERAGING TECHNOLOGY FOR BUSINESS GROWTH & EFFICIENCY

THE BEFORE: "JUST THROW IT IN THE DUMPSTER"

Dave wasn't exactly a tech guy. He had a system, or at least, that's what he told himself. His website person had created a fairly sophisticated spreadsheet to track leads, and for a while, that seemed good enough.

But as his business grew, things started slipping through the cracks.

His office manager, Diane, was the first to sound the alarm.

"Dave, I just called Mrs. Reynolds about her panel upgrade," she sighed, rubbing her temples. "Turns out, she was expecting me to be calling about a separate project at her rental property. She was so confused that I nearly had to convince her I wasn't running a scam."

Dave frowned. "So we mixed up two jobs. It happens."

Diane folded her arms. "It happens a lot. And that's just what I *catch* before it turns into a disaster. The spreadsheets aren't cutting it anymore. Every time we enter a repeat customer, it creates a new record instead of updating the existing one. We've got the same clients in the system *three* different times, and no one knows which project is which. It's making us look unprofessional."

Dave opened his mouth to argue, but she cut him off.

"Remember last week when I scheduled a crew for what I thought was a new service call? Turns out it was a warranty follow-up that should've been free, but we invoiced them. The customer called furious, thinking we were double-dipping."

Dave ran a hand over his face. "Okay, so we need better tracking..."

Diane smirked. "Oh, it gets better. The other day, I almost sent a follow-up email to a *closed* deal because the spreadsheet didn't update when the job was completed. It makes us look like we don't know what we're doing. And don't even get me started on scheduling mistakes. If I had a dollar for every time we double-booked a crew because our 'system' didn't show real-time availability, I could retire."

Then, just to prove Leslie's point, Dave decided to personally make a couple of calls.

First up: Peterson Manufacturing.

"Hey, Jim! Just checking in on that new panel install you wanted. I will get you that quote by end of day."

A pause. Then, a very confused Jim replied, "Dave... we closed that ticket out two weeks ago. I already paid the invoice."

Facepalm.

Next up: Lakeside Apartments.

"Hey, Ms. Daniels! I just wanted to follow up on your lighting retrofit project."

Another awkward pause. "Uh, Dave, I appreciate the check-in, but the work isn't even scheduled yet. We're still waiting on you guys to finalize the quote."

Double facepalm.

Diane gave him a pointed look. "Dave, we need a real CRM.

I'm spending half my day trying to piece together conversations across five different systems."

Dave grumbled. Spreadsheets had worked just fine for years. But deep down, he knew she was right. He was getting in his own way...again.

THE SHIFT: FROM CHAOS TO CLARITY

When Dave finally took the leap and implemented a real CRM, the changes were almost immediate. His new system:

Centralized Customer Data – Every job, every conversation, every project was now in one place.

Eliminated Embarrassing Client Confusion – His team could see a full client history instead of making cringeworthy mix-ups.

Automated Scheduling & Follow-ups – No more dropped balls. Clients were reminded about their appointments without Leslie having to manually chase them down.

Integrated Everything with Zapier – His CRM talked to his accounting software, his scheduling app, and even his email marketing tool.

Then came the real game-changer: dashboards.

"Diane," Dave said, staring at his computer screen in disbelief, "I can see my whole business at a glance. This is sorcery."

Instead of sorting through a dozen different spreadsheets, he had one place where he could track:

- Open jobs and their progress
- Monthly revenue projections
- Pending quotes and follow-ups
- Technician availability and workload
- Recurring maintenance contracts and their renewal dates

THE PAYOFF: RUNNING THE BUSINESS FROM THE BLEACHERS

A few months later, Dave found himself sitting in the bleachers of his daughter's cheer competition, laptop open, running a production meeting virtually.

With his dashboard pulled up, he could see every critical number in real time. Every job in progress, every open ticket, every pending estimate.

"Alright, guys," he said, slipping his noise-canceling headphones over his ears, shouting into his mic a little louder than necessary because the gym was deafening. "We've got six jobs in progress today. Mike, your crew is on the commercial build-out downtown. Diane, we've got an estimate follow-up pending for that restaurant remodel."

"Hey Dave," Mike interrupted, "we just got a booking request from a new client for an EV charger install. Looks like it came through the website form."

Dave clicked a tab, found the new lead in his CRM, and assigned it to the right technician, on the spot.

Instead of scrambling between job sites or calling in for status updates, he had every detail at his fingertips, from project timelines to open invoices.

Then, just as the team wrapped up their call, his daughter's team took the floor. Dave snapped his laptop shut, smiled, and cheered her on.

For the first time in forever, Dave felt like he was actually running his business instead of it running him. And more importantly, he wasn't missing out on his daughter's big moment.

THE TAKEAWAY: DO YOUR TOOLS SUPPORT YOUR GOALS?

Here's the thing: Technology isn't about replacing people, it's about empowering them.

Dave's story proves that when you implement the right systems, you don't just increase efficiency, you gain something even more valuable: time.

Time to grow your business instead of constantly putting out fires.

Time to actually lead instead of micromanage.

Time to be present for the moments that matter.

So if you're still clinging to spreadsheets and Post-it notes, ask yourself:

Are you running your business, or is your business running you?

Would your team (and your clients) be better off with a real system in place?

What could you do with the extra time technology could give you?

Because at the end of the day, the real Legacy Link isn't just about building a business, it's about building a business that supports your life, not the other way around.

CHAPTER 23

THE HEART OF SERVICE
LEADERSHIP IN SERVICE-BASED BUSINESSES

Dave Connelly thought he was a good boss. He paid his guys well. He stayed involved in every job. He worked harder than anyone. So why the hell couldn't he keep foremen?

He was on his third in two years, and this morning, Mike, his best guy, the one he actually trusted, had stormed into his office, slammed the door, and let loose.

THE MOMENT EVERYTHING CHANGED

"Do you have any idea what it's like to work for you?" Mike said, arms crossed, jaw tight.

Dave leaned back, frowning. "I pay you guys well. I show up to every site. I make sure the work gets done right. What more do you want?"

Mike laughed, but there was no humor in it. "Yeah, you show up, alright. That's half the problem. You don't lead, Dave. You hover. You criticize. You second-guess us every damn day. And then you wonder why your foremen quit."

Dave stiffened. "I don't second-guess."

"Bull. You don't trust anybody but yourself. And you know what? The last guy who walked out? You wanna know what he told me before he left?"

Dave didn't answer. He already knew he wouldn't like it.

Mike's voice was steel. "He said foremen don't actually lead on your jobs, they babysit you. Because you show up, bark ridiculous orders like a toddler, and then get in the way. You refuse to hand off real responsibility. And when things go wrong, it's never your fault."

Dave's stomach turned.

"And you know what?" Mike's voice dropped, but his eyes burned. "He was right."

Dave opened his mouth, but he had nothing. Maybe that was true.

THE LEADERSHIP CRISIS

Dave wanted to brush it off. Mike was just having a bad day. The guys didn't understand the pressure of owning a business. They didn't see the late nights, the payroll stress, the constant weight of making sure everyone got paid, including them.

But the words stuck with him.

That afternoon, Dave went to a job site to check on his newest foreman, Kyle.

Kyle was green but eager. He had potential. He reminded Dave of himself back when he was first starting out: hungry, willing to work his ass off. And Dave liked that about him.

As he walked onto the site, he immediately noticed Kyle handling things. Good. That's what he was supposed to do.

"Jason, why didn't you drill that hole where I told you?" Kyle barked at one of the guys.

"Because I had to adjust for the conduit."

"I didn't ask for an excuse. Just do what I said."

Jason clenched his jaw. Dave caught the quick flash of frustration in his eyes before he muttered something under his breath and got back to work.

Kyle turned his attention to another tech, sighing loudly. *"You need to move faster, man. This isn't break time."*

Dave frowned. He hadn't noticed it before, but now he felt it. The crew's energy was off.

The guys weren't moving with their usual rhythm. They were stiff. Avoiding eye contact. They weren't working as a team; they were working ... to avoid Kyle.

And that's when it hit him.

Kyle wasn't leading.

He was controlling.

He was micromanaging.

And Dave had taught him to do it.

The realization was nauseating.

He had always prided himself on being a tough but fair leader. But was he just tough and not fair at all? Had he actually taught his guys how to lead, or just how to bark orders louder?

And if that was the case... how much damage had he done?

THE HARDEST QUESTION OF ALL

That night, Dave sat on his back porch, staring at the sky. His wife, Lisa, sat next to him, sipping her tea.

"You're awful quiet," she said.

He sighed. *"Mike lit me up today. Said I don't trust anyone, that I'm burning myself out and driving my team away."*

Lisa studied him for a long moment. *"Well... is he wrong?"*

Dave chuckled bitterly. *"You're supposed to be on my side."*

"I am on your side. But your side should be winning, not working yourself into an early grave."

Silence.

Dave took a long sip of his beer. *"Kyle's turning into me,"* he admitted.

Lisa tilted her head. *"What do you mean?"*

"I went to the site today. He's running jobs exactly like I do. Short-tempered. No patience. Taking over instead of teaching." He exhaled. *"I watched him suck the life out of his guys. And I realized... I do the exact same thing."*

Lisa was quiet for a moment. Then, softly, she said, *"So what are you going to do about it?"*

And for the first time in his life, Dave didn't have an answer.

THE CATALYST FOR CHANGE

The next morning, still reeling from yesterday's revelations, Dave met up with his old friend, Shane, who had recently sold him some legal insurance. Over coffee, their conversation drifted to leadership challenges.

"You know, Dave," Shane said, reaching into his bag, "I've been reading this book that might resonate with you." He handed over a copy of *Real Leadership: 9 Simple Practices for Leading and Living with Purpose* by John Addison.

Dave glanced at the cover, intrigued. "Thanks, Shane. I'll give it a look."

Later that night, sitting in his favorite chair, Dave opened the book. The introduction grabbed him immediately:

"A mediocre leader tries to impress people with how important he or she is. A great leader impresses upon people how important they are."

Dave felt a pang of recognition. He had been so focused on asserting his authority that he had overlooked the importance of empowering his team.

As he delved deeper, he encountered Addison's nine leadership practices:

1. Decide Who You Are: Clarify your values and stand firm in them.
2. Shine Your Light on Others: Celebrate your team's achievements rather than your own.
3. Build on Your Strengths: Focus on what you do best and delegate the rest.
4. Earn Your Position: Lead by example and gain respect through actions.
5. Focus on What You Can Control: Direct your energy toward areas where you can make a difference.
6. Develop a Peaceful Core: Maintain calmness to navigate challenges effectively.
7. Be a Lighthouse: Provide guidance and remain steadfast during turbulent times.
8. Don't Burn Bridges: Preserve relationships, even when disagreements arise.
9. Make Your Parents Proud: Act with integrity in all endeavors.

Each principle felt like a direct challenge to his current approach. He realized he had no idea how to lead. Hell, he had no idea what a leader was. His foundation was someone Just. Like. Him. Whoa, that realization was as unpleasant as they come.

One passage struck him deeply:

"There's a big difference between a problem and a situation. If writing a check or making some kind of adjustment to what you're doing can fix it, then it's not a problem. It's a situation."

Dave pondered this. He had been treating every issue as a monumental problem, creating unnecessary stress for himself and his team.

Closing the book, Dave felt a mix of shame and hope. He recognized his shortcomings but also saw a path forward. He wasn't there yet, not by a long shot. But for the first time, he felt he had the tools to become the leader he aspired to be.

DAVE'S FIRST (RELUCTANT) STEPS INTO REAL LEADERSHIP

The next morning, Dave walked into the shop, *Real Leadership* tucked under his arm. He didn't want to talk about it. He sure as hell didn't want anyone knowing he was reading *a damn leadership book*. But Mike had called him out, Lisa had backed him up, and somewhere in his gut, he knew they were right.

He needed to change.

He just didn't know how...yet.

His first test came sooner than expected.

Kyle was already at the job site, snapping at Jason over a minor adjustment.

"That's not where I told you to put it," Kyle barked.

Jason sighed. "I adjusted for the .... ,"

"I didn't ask for an excuse."

Jason's jaw tightened. The rest of the crew kept their heads down, avoiding Kyle altogether.

Dave felt the tension. *Damn. I've seen this before.* He frowned, crossing his arms.

Dave exhaled sharply. "Kyle, walk with me."

Kyle stiffened, then nodded, following him a few steps away from the crew. "Everything okay, boss?"

Dave wasn't great at these conversations. Hell, he wasn't even sure what he was about to say. But he knew he couldn't ignore it.

"Kyle, you remind me of me," Dave said, voice flat. "And ... that's .... Not ... a compliment."

Kyle frowned. "I, what?"

Dave scrubbed a hand over his face. "I've been running things a certain way for a long time. Bark orders, demand perfection, push harder. And I thought that was leadership. Turns out, it's just being a controlling pain in the ass."

Kyle's jaw twitched, but he stayed quiet.

"I taught you to run jobs this way," Dave continued. "I set this example. And now I'm seeing exactly where that gets us."

Kyle shifted his weight. "So... what do I do instead?"

Dave hesitated. He wasn't used to admitting he didn't have all the answers.

"I don't know," he admitted. "Not yet. But I'm figuring it out. And you and I are gonna figure it out together."

Kyle swallowed. He still looked uncertain, like he wasn't sure if this was some kind of test.

Dave sighed, looking back at the crew. "Start with this: Ask Jason *why* he adjusted that conduit. Instead of assuming he screwed up, assume he was thinking ahead. If he actually did mess up, you'll still get there. But maybe, just maybe, he was trying to do his job right, and you just didn't see it yet."

Kyle looked back at Jason, who was still working, jaw tight, shoulders stiff.

Dave clapped Kyle on the shoulder, a little heavier than necessary. "Go on."

Kyle took a slow breath, then walked back toward the crew.

Dave didn't follow. He wasn't there to micromanage. He was here to learn.

For the first time, he *wanted* to learn.

THE LEGACY OF LEADERSHIP ISN'T INSTANT

Dave didn't leave that site feeling like a whole new man. Hell, he still had a long way to go. He'd probably still screw it up. But for the first time, he *saw* the problem.

Kyle was his mirror.

And if he didn't like what he saw?

It was up to him to change it, and help Kyle, too.

FINAL THOUGHT: THE LEGACY YOU LEAVE

Dave hadn't figured it all out.

He probably never would.

But he finally saw the problem. And that meant he could do something about it.

Leadership isn't about control. It's about influence. And here's the kicker, you're leading, whether you mean to or not.

Every time Dave barked at his guys, micromanaged a job, or refused to trust his team, he was *teaching* them how to lead.

And now?

He had to ask himself a brutal question:

If the people working under you start leading just like you...

Is that a good thing?

Because whether you like it or not, that's your legacy.

That's the Legacy Link.

And whether that link holds strong, or snaps under pressure, depends entirely on the kind of leader you decide to be today.

And ... Dave wasn't remotely there yet.

But something had shifted.

For the first time, he wasn't just frustrated with his crew, he was frustrated with himself.

Kyle wasn't the problem. Neither was Mike.

The problem was the example *he* had set.

And that meant he was the only one who could fix it.

But how?

He rubbed a hand over his face, staring at his own reflection in the rearview mirror of his truck. He looked tired. Older. Worn the hell out.

For years, he'd thought the only way to get ahead was to push harder. To demand perfection. To be in control.

But maybe... maybe control wasn't leadership.

Maybe fear was the root of the problem?

A sinking feeling settled in his gut as he thought about his crew. How many of them felt like Kyle did?

How many of them, right now, were working through gritted teeth, just counting the days until they could leave?

How many more guys was he going to lose before he figured this out?

The thought twisted in his stomach.

He didn't have an answer.

But tomorrow, he was going to find out.

The hard way.

WHY THIS MATTERS FOR YOU

Dave's wake-up call isn't just his.

It's happening in businesses just like yours every single day.

The question isn't *whether* you're teaching leadership.

It's what kind of leadership you're teaching.

Are you building leaders, or just more task-runners?

Does your team take ownership, or do they just obey orders?

If you weren't here tomorrow, would they step up, or step away?

One day, you won't be at the helm anymore.

And what you leave behind? That's your real legacy.

It's time to wake up.

CHAPTER 24

LEADERSHIP IS A VERB

THE BREAKING POINT

It started, as most bad days do, with something small.

Brent had just finished a complex conduit run for a high-end retail renovation, one of the biggest jobs they'd landed this quarter. It was clean. Precise. Perfect. Well, he thought it was.

Dave walked over, squinted at the setup, and let out a long, exaggerated sigh.

"These bends are ... fine, I guess," he muttered. "But not how I would do them."

Brent froze. He'd worked his ass off on that job, spent hours making sure the bends were tight, efficient, beautiful. His body stiffened as Dave crouched down and pointed at one connection.

"You should've used a back-to-back here instead of a saddle. Would've saved a few inches of conduit."

The *old* Dave would have ripped into him for every tiny imperfection. But today? Today, something was off. Dave sounded... hesitant.

Brent exhaled sharply, his patience fraying. "Dave, that's code-compliant. It's clean. It works. The inspector already signed off on it."

Dave waved a dismissive hand. "I'm just saying. If you want to be great, you don't settle for good enough."

"It's not 'good enough,' the inspector said it was damn near perfect," Brent snapped.

Dave saw his opening. "Yeah, damn near... is not perfect, Brent. These could have been better and used less material. If they weren't signed off, I'd make you redo them."

"Oh, because that wouldn't waste conduit at all, huh?" Brent shot back.

"If I say we waste it, then we waste it. It's my damn checkbook. If you waste it... "

That was it. That was the moment.

Before Dave could finish, Brent ripped off his gloves, tossing them onto his tool bag. The other guys on the crew went dead silent. Even Mike, who had been listening from across the room, stopped mid-drill.

Brent wiped the sweat off his forehead, looked Dave in the eye, and made the decision right there.

"I'm done."

Dave blinked. "What?"

"I'm done," Brent repeated. "I can't work like this anymore. I do everything by the book, I bust my ass, and it's never good enough for you."

Dave scoffed. "Oh, come on, Brent. You're overreacting." But Dave knew it, in the pit of his stomach, he knew this was on him. He mentally counted at least five ass-chewings he'd given Brent in the last month over minor things ... all in the name of "teaching him". He wasn't a leader, he was a jackass. And, he knew it.

"No, I'm done. I'm done giving a damn. I'm done caring more about this business than you care about your own people."

He grabbed his tool bag and turned toward the door.

Dave was trying to find words to say, but nothing would come out, and before he could utter a sound, Brent spoke for them both.

"You know what? Nelson Electric offered me a job last week. They offered to pay for my journeyman test. They gave me FREE study materials and told me if I passed, I'd have my own truck and an apprentice by next month."

Dave's stomach plummeted.

Brent? At Nelson? Their biggest competitor?

And just like that, he was gone.

Dave stood there, stunned.

The room was silent until Mike broke it wide open.

MIKE LIGHTS HIM UP, AGAIN

Mike didn't even wait for Brent to fully clear the door before he unleashed.

"ARE YOU HAPPY NOW?!" His voice ricocheted off the metal studs.

Dave turned toward him, still dazed. "Mike, I..."

"No. Shut up." Mike stalked forward, his eyes blazing. "Do you even realize what just happened?! You just trained your biggest competitor's new star electrician. You took a guy who was loyal as hell, poured knowledge into him, and then drove him straight into Nelson's damn arms! AGAIN!"

Dave's face darkened. "I didn't..."

"You didn't?!" Mike laughed bitterly. "You sure as hell did! You ran him off! And for what? A damn conduit bend?! And, as good of one as I've ever seen you do!!"

Dave clenched his fists, his anger building. "I was just giving feedback."

"That wasn't feedback. That was straight-up bullshit. Just your ego out on a walk." Mike shook his head, disgusted. "You nitpick everything because it's the only thing that makes you feel like you belong here."

Dave's breath hitched. "Excuse me?"

"I didn't stutter." Mike didn't flinch. "You know you are just winging running this company. You know you run off good people. So instead of fixing it, you double down on being the best damn electrician in the room. That's all you've got, isn't it? The technical skill. Because if you're not the best at that, what the hell are you?"

Dave opened his mouth. Nothing came out.

Mike exhaled, shaking his head. "I can't do this anymore, man. I've watched you push people out of here for years. I stuck around because I kept thinking you'd wake up and change. But I can't keep carrying this place on my back while you act like you're Marvel's newest and lamest Avenger."

He turned, grabbing his jacket. "If you need me, I'll be at Nelson's seeing if they've got room for a washed-up foreman."

The door slammed.

Dave stood there, his face burning, his hands shaking.

Mike had never threatened to leave before.

And, the reality of what he'd learned in the last few days rained down like daggers from God himself. If Mike left, the business would suffer immensely. Dave might not be able to replace him, at least not quickly.

THE SUPPLIER HQ VISIT & TOM'S LUNCH

The next morning, Dave didn't show up to the job site.

He felt like quitting. He wasn't even sure what he was doing. But he needed... something.

Mike must have known, because around noon, he popped into Dave's office and tossed him his jacket.

"Get in the truck. We're going for a drive."

Dave didn't argue. He was so relieved to see Mike there, he might have followed him through the gates of hell ... and that's kinda what happened.

They ended up at Lighting Solutions Co., one of their main suppliers.

The moment Dave stepped inside, he knew something was different. This wasn't like any supplier's office he'd ever seen.

Employees were *laughing*. The front desk receptionist high-fived a warehouse worker.

People actually *liked* working here.

That's when he met Tom Masters, the CEO, a sharp-eyed guy in his 60s who didn't waste time with pleasantries.

"Mike says you're an ass," Tom said, smirking.

Dave blinked. "Uh..."

"He also says you're *not beyond saving*." Tom walked past him toward the front door. "Let's get lunch."

At lunch, Tom *tore him apart*.

THE WAKE-UP CALL FROM TOM

"You're playing *small*," Tom said, swirling his coffee.

Dave frowned. "I built this business. "

"Yeah, yeah, you *worked* for it. You *earned* it. You know what else you did? You made it *miserable* for everyone else."

Dave stiffened. "I pay my guys well."

"And yet, they're leaving. *Why do you think that is?*"

Dave had nothing.

Tom leaned back. "I'll tell you why. You're out here running a business like it's just a bigger version of your one-man show. But newsflash, *you're not an electrician anymore. You're a leader*. And you're a bad one."

Dave exhaled. "How do I fix it?"

Tom chuckled. "You can start by realizing you don't know sh*t."

Dave scowled. "Thanks for that."

"Don't mention it," Tom smirked. "Listen, I can introduce you to someone who taught *me* how to lead. But he won't take it easy on you."

Dave hesitated.

"You can keep pretending you have it all figured out," Tom said, tossing cash on the table, "or you can actually *learn* something."

Dave sighed. "Fine. Who is he?"

Tom grinned. "Frank Dawson. He's gonna make you hate your life for a while. But trust me, you'll thank me later."

THE TURNING POINT: MEETING FRANK DAWSON

True to his word, Tom introduced Dave to Frank Dawson, which led to a golf game.

Frank was Mike on steroids. By the ninth hole, Dave wasn't sure if Frank was gonna hit his next shot, or *wrap his driver around his skull.*

"You think your business is special?" Frank asked, lining up his putt.

Dave frowned. "Well... yeah."

Frank sunk the putt, smirking.

"It's *not*."

Dave scowled. "Excuse me?"

"It's. Not. Special." Frank turned to face him. "Every business runs on two things: leadership and culture. And if you're bleeding people? If your best guys are leaving? Then it's not a business, it's a *hostage situation*."

Dave winced.

Frank wasn't done.

"You wanna fix it? You stop being the problem."

Dave stared down at his club, turning it in his hands.

For the first time, he shut up.

And for the next two months, Frank ripped him apart and rebuilt him.

CHAPTER 25
CULTURE SHIFTS & BBQ

THE AFTERMATH

The two months after meeting Frank Dawson were brutal.

Frank didn't just talk about leadership, he shoved it down Dave's throat.

It wasn't theoretical. It wasn't a bunch of feel-good corporate fluff. It was gut-punching reality checks followed by actionable steps that made Dave wish he could crawl into a hole and disappear.

Frank had Dave shadow other business owners, guys who had built companies that ran without them. Leaders who didn't hover, who didn't micromanage, who had built real culture.

And at every turn, Dave saw the contrast.

He saw how he had been doing it wrong.

Saw how every successful business had the one thing his company didn't.

Buy-in.

THE LESSON THAT NEARLY BROKE HIM

It was at a construction site for a large electrical contractor when the final hammer fell.

Frank had taken him to watch a foreman run a job. Not a business owner, just a guy leading a crew.

And the difference was *night and day*.

The foreman, Terry, approached a group of apprentices. One of them had messed up a wire pull, badly.

Dave braced himself for the inevitable dressing down.

But instead, Terry crouched down next to the kid, pointed at the mess, and said, "Alright, let's figure this out together."

No yelling. No sighing. No berating.

Just teaching.

The kid nodded, relieved. The tension evaporated. And within minutes, the problem was solved.

Dave felt sick.

Because he had never once handled things like that.

Instead, he had become the guy everyone was afraid to disappoint.

And not because they respected him.

Because they feared him.

Frank didn't say a word the entire drive back.

Dave didn't either.

Because he wasn't sure he could speak without his voice breaking.

THE PLAN: IF YOU WANT DIFFERENT RESULTS, YOU HAVE TO LEAD DIFFERENTLY

The first thing Dave did?

Nothing.

For the first time in his life, he left people the hell alone.

No nitpicking. No micromanaging. He let Mike and Leslie actually run the day-to-day.

At first, his team was skeptical. They were waiting for the other shoe to drop.

But it didn't.

Then, he started implementing real changes.

He started shopping for full benefits packages for his full-time people.

He and Lisa started doing the math on how profit sharing could work.

He asked Frank to help him put together a leadership training program for the jump from journeyman to foreman, and beyond.

But one thing still nagged at him.

Brent.

Dave stared at his phone.

The contact list was open. Brent's name was right there.

He tapped it once. The call button hovered under his thumb.

Then, he locked the screen and tossed the phone on his desk.

This was stupid.

Brent had already moved on. He had a better offer. A better future. What the hell was dinner going to do?

His brow furrowed as he felt a pang of guilt. Maybe Mike was right. Maybe this wasn't fixable.

His phone buzzed. A text from Mike.

Did you call him yet?

Dave exhaled, rubbing his face. He should have known Mike wouldn't let this go.

Another buzz.

I swear to God, if you don't, I'll do it myself.

Dave let out a sharp breath, picked up his phone, and dialed before he could overthink it.

It rang twice. Then,

"Hey, Dave." Brent's voice was neutral. Guarded.

Dave cleared his throat. Too late to back out now.

"Hey Brent, I was wondering if you'd be willing to meet me for dinner at Lucy's one night soon, my treat," Dave blurted out before he could chicken out.

Silence.

Then, "Um, I... guess... so." Brent replied, the hesitation in his voice rivaling a man trying to defuse a bomb with a YouTube tutorial.

Dave exhaled. "Great. Friday at seven?"

Brent still sounded suspicious. "What's this about?"

Dave ran a hand over his face. "Just dinner. No catch. No lecture. Just... a conversation."

Brent paused. Then sighed. "Alright. But just so you know, if this turns into some motivational speech, I'm ordering the tomahawk steak on your dime."

Dave smirked. "Fair enough. See you Friday."

Brent was confused, sure. But he wasn't about to turn down a free steak from Lucy's. And besides, Dave wasn't his boss anymore.

So what the hell.

THE APOLOGY THAT ACTUALLY MATTERED

Over steak and mashed potatoes, Dave did something else he'd never done.

He apologized.

Not a half-assed, "Hey, man, sorry about that." Not a "Sorry you felt that way."

A real apology.

He owned it.

Dave sat in the steakhouse, waiting. His leg bounced under the table. He'd been in uncomfortable situations before; hell, he made a habit of putting his employees in them.

But this? This was a different kind of discomfort.

Because tonight, he wasn't the boss. He was a man who had screwed up and had to own it.

The door swung open, and there was Brent. His expression was guarded, but he sat down. "Alright. Let's hear it."

Dave exhaled. *"I owe you an apology."*

Brent blinked then laughed nervously, his flabbers completely ghasted. *"That's a first."* He muttered as he looked around for cameras. Was this a prank? Was he unwittingly on some reality show?

Dave didn't deflect. Didn't argue.

"I was too hard on you," he admitted, his voice rough. *"I saw something in you I never saw in myself, natural leadership. And that scared the hell out of me."*

Brent's eyebrows lifted. *"You? Scared?"*

"Yeah, kid. I was terrified. Because I knew you were everything I was and all that I am not. I didn't build you up, I tore you down."

Brent stared at him for a long moment. "I never wanted to leave, Dave."

Dave's throat tightened.

Brent continued. "Yeah, you were rough and nitpicky, but you're a really good teacher when you're actually teaching a concept. You're smart as hell. I respect your talent and knowledge."

Dave looked him in the eye, surprised but touched to his core.

"Then come back," Dave said. "And this time, I promise, I'll give you a reason to stay."

Brent smirked. "I don't even think you're a bad leader. I just think you get in your own way a lot. And you're cocky as hell."

Dave grinned. "Yeah. That's fair."

Brent raised an eyebrow. "You're buying dessert, right?"

Dave laughed. "Damn right."

A few weeks later, Dave did something unheard of.

He shut the business down on a Friday.

Not for maintenance. Not for training.

For a reset.

A day on the lake.

Three pontoon boats. His entire team. No work talk allowed.

For the first time in years, Dave wasn't thinking about schedules, deadlines, or profit margins.

Mike was floating in an inner tube, beer in hand, grumbling about how the younger guys relied too much on laser levels.

Diane had somehow commandeered the Bluetooth speaker, bouncing between classic rock and whatever new-age techno mess the apprentices requested.

And Brent? Brent was back.

Watching the guys joke and laugh, Dave felt something shift in his gut.

This wasn't just a team-building exercise.

This was an unspoken truce.

Now, it was time for him to say what needed to be said.

THE TALK THAT CHANGED EVERYTHING

Dave stood up on the boat, cleared his throat, and immediately regretted not preparing a speech.

Everyone turned, half-expecting him to yell about a job site.

Instead, he rubbed the back of his neck, awkward but determined.

"Alright, listen up." His voice was rough but steady. *"I've been a hard-ass for a long time. I've nitpicked, micromanaged, and run damn good people out of this company."*

He glanced at Brent.

"Some of them almost for good."

Brent smirked.

Dave swallowed, looking at Mike.

"And I've had ... people, better men than me, *waiting for me to wake the hell up.*"

Mike raised an eyebrow but said nothing.

Dave took a deep breath.

"I want you all to know something. I see it now. And I hate that it took losing people, almost losing *all of you,* to realize it."

He looked around at his team. These guys weren't just employees.

They were his business.

"You are what makes this company work. Not me. Not my skills. Not my name on the damn paperwork. You."

He let that hang for a moment before continuing.

"I can't change overnight. But I can start today."

He pulled a folded piece of paper from his pocket.

"This isn't just some 'thanks for sticking around' speech. This is a real plan. Lisa and I have been working on this for the last few weeks. Diane knew about it, but that's it. Here's what's changing."

A real benefits package. Full health insurance, life insurance, disability insurance, 14 days of PTO, and paid holidays.

A profit-sharing plan. When the company wins, everyone wins.

A leadership training program. This is for anyone, but it's especially for journeymen before they get promoted to foreman.

And a 15-year plan for someone, maybe Brent, to take over.

Dave sighed.

"Or maybe someone else. Maybe it's one of you apprentices right now. But this company is going to outlive me. That starts today."

Silence.

Then, a low whistle from one of the apprentices. "Did he just say... profit-sharing?"

Diane squinted like she didn't trust it. "Wait. Hold on. You were serious!?"

Dave nodded. "Dead serious."

Brent tilted his head. "What's the catch?"

Dave let out a sharp breath. "No catch. Just overdue."

The crew broke into chuckles. The tension started to ease, but Dave saw something else, too. Hope.

Like maybe, just maybe, this wasn't all talk.

Then, Mike climbed up on the boat with Dave.

He looked at Dave long and hard, arms crossed.

Then he smirked. *"I don't totally hate this."*

The crew laughed.

Dave rolled his eyes. *"Good. Because I've got one more thing."*

He pulled an envelope from his back pocket and tossed it to Mike.

Mike caught it, frowning as he tore it open.

His eyes widened.

"Box seats," Dave said, grinning. *"For the Falcons."*

Mike's mouth opened. *"Are you shittin' me?"*

Dave laughed. *"I know, I know. You deserve a better team. But it's also an extra week off, with pay."*

Mike blinked.

Dave shrugged. *"For not killing me."*

The crew erupted into cheers.

Mike shook his head, but he was smiling.

Brent raised his beer. *"To not killing Dave!"*

"To not killing Dave!" the team echoed, laughing as they clinked bottles and cans together.

And for the first time in his entire damn life, Dave knew, without a doubt, this wasn't just his company anymore.

It was theirs.

FINAL THOUGHT: CULTURE IS EVERYTHING

That night, as the sun set over the water, Dave sat back, arms crossed, watching his team.

His family.

He had learned from Frank that your team *can* feel like family, so long as you don't put family-style expectations on them.

Mike was laughing at something Brent said. Diane had somehow convinced the apprentices to sing along to a ridiculous pop song.

They weren't just here for a paycheck.

They were here because they wanted to be.

And for the first time, Dave understood what real leadership looked like.

Legacy isn't built in a day.

But it can be lost in one.

Culture is everything.

WHY THIS MATTERS FOR YOU

Dave didn't transform overnight.

Neither will you.

If your team is struggling, you might be the problem.

If your business is bleeding good people, your leadership needs work.

If your company feels like a revolving door, your culture is broken.

But here's the thing: You can fix it.

Culture isn't built by accident. It's built with intentional leadership.

So take a hard look at your team.

Would they stay if they had another offer?

Would they *want* to?

Because if your culture is built on fear, control, or microman-agement, you don't have a team.

You have hostages.

And one day, they'll escape.

Build a business people want to stay in.

Build a legacy worth leading.

It starts today.

CHAPTER 26

REPUTATION IS EVERYTHING

BEYOND THE SALE

THE MAN WHO DIDN'T NEED MARKETING, UNTIL HE DID

For years, Elliot Shaw never had to lift a finger when it came to marketing. He ran Shaw Custom Woodworks, a high-end cabinetry and furniture company that catered to luxury homeowners and boutique hotels. His craftsmanship was second to none, and his name carried weight in the industry.

People didn't just hire Elliot, they waited months for a chance to work with him.

Interior designers swore by him.

General contractors referred him without hesitation.

Clients raved about his work, sending their friends his way.

He never ran ads. Never posted on social media. Never even thought about hiring a sales team.

Why would he?

His reputation was enough.

Until it wasn't.

One year, the referrals slowed. Not overnight, but noticeably.

Calls that once came in daily dropped to a few a week. Then a few a month.

And Elliot?

He chalked it up to a slow season...until it wasn't just a season anymore.

"What the hell is going on?" he asked his wife one night, frustration thick in his voice. "I haven't changed anything! I still do the best work in town!"

Vanessa sighed and set her wine glass down. "Elliot... have you looked around lately?"

"What's that supposed to mean?"

"It means," she said, choosing her words carefully, "that you've spent the last twenty years building a business based on your name, but you haven't done anything to stay relevant."

He scowled. "I do quality work. That's all that should matter."

Vanessa shook her head. "Elliot, I love you, but wake up. There are dozens of guys out there doing great work. But now? They're posting their projects, sharing their process, and showing up on Instagram, LinkedIn, and even TikTok."

Elliot scoffed. "I don't have time for social media."

Vanessa shrugged. "You might want to make time. Because right now? People are forgetting you exist."

OUCH, forgetting he existed ... after all the artistry and relationships. That was tough to hear.

Elliot had built his business on word-of-mouth and reputation, but he never built a system to keep that reputation alive.

The world moved forward. He didn't. And now, his once-thriving business was fading from relevance.

He needed a plan. Fast.

BEYOND THE SALE: WHAT IT MEANS TO BUILD A REPUTATION THAT LASTS

Elliot's story isn't unique.

Thousands of businesses, maybe even yours, run almost exclusively on reputation and referrals.

And while that's a powerful foundation, it's not enough to sustain a business forever.

Here's the truth:

Reputation is NOT static. It's either growing or dying.

Your best work won't market itself forever. You need to keep reminding people why you're the best.

Referrals are a gift, not a strategy. And gifts can stop coming.

So, how do you build a business that keeps its reputation strong, even when you're not actively in the room shaking hands?

The answer?

You anchor yourself in something bigger than just good work.

You build a legacy.

THE COMPANIES THAT BUILT SOMETHING BIGGER THAN THEMSELVES

Take TOMS Shoes.

For years, their brand wasn't just about selling shoes, it was about their One-for-One Giving Model. Buy a pair, and they'd donate a pair to someone in need.

Did it explode their brand?

Yes.

Did it make them memorable, even beyond their product?

Absolutely.

Or look at Patagonia.

They built a brand not just on great gear, but on environmental activism. They take a bold stance on sustainability, donate millions to conservation efforts, and even encourage customers NOT to buy new products unless they really need them.

And guess what?

They're one of the most respected and loyalty-driven brands in the world.

But it's not just the big guys.

Small businesses do this every single day.

A coffee company in Guatemala partners with non-profits, donating proceeds to local charities and supporting ethical farming practices.

A local mechanic who doesn't just fix cars, he mentors at-risk teens and teaches them auto repair to help them find careers.

A plumbing company that sponsors Little League teams, hosts free community workshops, and helps homeowners prepare for winter storms.

What do they all have in common?

They built reputations that go beyond the sale.

HOW TO BECOME THE BUSINESS EVERYONE TALKS ABOUT (FOR THE RIGHT REASONS)

If you want to stay relevant, you have to make sure your business isn't just known for what it does, but what it stands for.

Elliot figured this out, eventually.

After sulking for a few weeks (and Vanessa threatening to start a TikTok account for him), he got serious about his reputation.

Here's what he did:

He started sharing his expertise online. Behind-the-scenes videos of his process. Time-lapses of his projects. Before-and-after shots that showed his skill.

He created a customer community. He built a VIP email list, offering exclusive home renovation tips and giving past clients first dibs on limited project slots.

He built a referral engine. Instead of waiting for word-of-mouth, he rewarded past clients for referrals, making it easy and rewarding to spread the word.

He aligned himself with a cause. He started donating a portion of every luxury kitchen remodel to a local nonprofit that builds housing for families in need.

And did he become the go-to name in his market again?

Yes.

But not "just like that."

Because here's what people forget:

Doing high-quality work *and* marketing your business both take effort.

The difference is, only one gets dropped the minute things get tight.

And it's almost always marketing.

But let's be real:

Without marketing?

There is no business.

For every action, there's an equal and opposite reaction.

If you cut off your visibility, you cut off your pipeline.

If you stop showing up, people stop thinking of you.

It's not rocket science. It's physics.

Elliot didn't just do great work.

He made sure people *knew* about it, and felt good being part of it.

Because people don't just want quality craftsmanship.

They want to hire someone they believe in.

They want to feel like their dollars are going toward something that matters.

They want to be part of something bigger.

THE LEGACY LINK: YOUR REPUTATION IS YOUR GREATEST ASSET

So, here's the real question:

What do people say about you when you're not in the room?

Not just about your work.

Not just about your customer service.

But about your impact.

If the answer is "They do great work," that's good.

But if the answer is "They're the best in town, and they actually give a damn," that's great.

That's legacy.

So, what's your next move?

How can you show up more in your community?

How can you make your business known for more than just the service you provide?

How can you ensure that your reputation doesn't just survive, but thrives?

Because at the end of the day, a great reputation isn't given.

It's built. Every single day.

And that?

That's the Legacy Link.

FINAL THOUGHT

Don't let your reputation be a thing of the past.

Make it something people talk about for generations.

Now, let's get to work.

CHAPTER 27

THE BUSINESS OF HELPING PEOPLE

FOR REAL

HELPING IS THE CORE OF BUSINESS

Let's strip business down to its simplest form: people need something, and you provide it. That's it.

Every business, whether you're fixing electrical systems, installing HVAC units, cutting hair, or designing websites, exists because you solve a problem. People are willing to pay you because they need your help. And if you do a good job? They tell other people. That's how businesses grow.

But here's the part many business owners miss:

You have an opportunity to do more than just the job.

You have the ability to create real, meaningful impact, not just for your customers, but for your community. And when you do that? You don't just build a business. You build a legacy.

GIVING, THE RIGHT WAY (AND THE WRONG WAY)

The idea of giving back gets tossed around a lot in business. Big corporations donate millions to charities. Small businesses sponsor

Little League teams. And then there's that guy on TikTok who pressure-washes people's driveways for free (and makes money from the creator fund doing it).

All of that is great.

But real, impactful giving? It's not about throwing money at a problem. It's about understanding the problem first.

Enter: The Wagon Story

My dad, Link, learned this the hard way when he was a teenager, working at a little gas station in the late '60s.

Every day, a young man with obvious special needs would come by, pulling the creakiest, ricketiest wagon you could imagine. You could hear him coming from a mile away. He picked up old soda bottles, cashed them in at the station, bought himself a drink and a candy bar, and then headed home, squeaky wagon in tow.

One day, Dad, trying to be helpful, said, "Hey, you want me to fix that wagon? I can get it rolling better for you."

The kid lit up. "Sure, mister, that'd be great!"

So Dad got to work. He straightened the axles, tightened the bolts, greased the wheels, and even fixed the handle. By the time he was done, that wagon was silent and smooth as butter.

The kid thanked him, grinning ear to ear, and rolled it home with ease.

The next day, Dad was at work when he saw the kid walking toward the store again, but with no wagon.

Dad frowned. "Hey, buddy, where's your wagon?"

The kid's eyes went wide. "Aw, man! That wagon went down my hill like a lightning streak! It was so fast I couldn't even see where I was going! I got scared and jumped off! The wagon's in a ditch. I don't think we can fix it now."

Dad just stood there, realizing exactly what had happened.

"Wait, you RODE it," he confirmed.

"Yep, I always ride it down the hill, it's fun ... and going fast was fun too ... but then it wasn't," the kid explained.

Dad had tried to help.

But instead of asking questions, like "Hey, do you take this down hills a lot?" he jumped in and 'fixed' something that didn't actually need fixing.

The result? The kid lost his wagon.

And Dad? Well, he never forgot the lesson: Before you help someone, make sure they actually need your help.

The Right Way to Make an Impact

That lesson isn't just a funny childhood story; it's a business principle.

How many times have you seen a business jump on a charity bandwagon without really knowing what they're supporting?

Or a company decide to "give back" in a way that's more about their image than actually helping people?

That's not real impact.

HOW DO YOU HELP PEOPLE FOR REAL?

1. Understand the Need First

Don't assume. Ask. What does your community actually need? What do your customers struggle with beyond just the service you provide?

2. Align It with Your Business

The best impact uses your strengths. If you run a bakery, giving out leftover bread to shelters makes sense. If you're a mechanic, hosting a free "Car Basics" class for single moms makes sense.

3. Make It Sustainable

Random acts of generosity are great, but building impact into your business model is even better.

4. Tell People (The Right Way)

It's okay to talk about how your business gives back. Just don't make it a PR stunt.

Instead of "Look how generous we are," the message should be:"This is important. Here's how we're trying to help. Join us."

YOUR BUSINESS, YOUR LEGACY

I've always believed in helping people. I got that from my dad.

Back when I published a horse magazine, I did everything I could to support horse rescues.

Today, I share my knowledge, for free, whenever I can.

If someone sits down with me to talk about their business, they don't walk away with a sales pitch. They walk away with clarity, an idea, a plan. I don't always tell them how to solve their problems, but I get them asking the right questions and looking in the right direction to suit their unique needs.

And here's the thing: That's good business.

The more you help, the more you become known for helping.

The more people see you not just as a service provider, but as someone who actually gives a damn, the better things will go. And not because you feign interest, but because you do give a damn.

And in the long run? That's what makes you unforgettable.

FINAL THOUGHT: HELP, BUT HELP RIGHT

Dave learned this lesson in Chapter 19. He built a better business by building up his people.

Jack figured it out with his maintenance contracts. He stopped just fixing things and started preventing problems before they happened.

I learned it from my dad and that damn runaway wagon.

So now, I'll ask you:

What's your wagon?

Where are you "fixing" things without really understanding the need?

Where could you be making a real difference, not just to boost your image, but because you actually give a damn?

Because that?

That's the Legacy Link.

CHAPTER 28

THE LEGACY LINK
CREATING TRANSFERABLE VALUE

The Legacy Link isn't just about building a business. It's about building something that lasts.

And if there's anything we've learned, from Link, from Dave, from Jack, from Sarah, it's that hard work alone won't secure your legacy. Systems do. Leadership does. People do.

THE MEN WHO BUILT SOMETHING

LINK HELMANDOLLAR: THE HARDEST WORKER IN THE ROOM

When you think about Link's life, you don't just think of an HVAC business. You think of a man. A provider. A craftsman who never cut corners, who never left a customer in the lurch.

For over three decades, Link built something real. A loyal customer base of 300 clients. A business generating $500,000 to $750,000 a year. A reputation so strong that people waited for him instead of calling someone else.

But when his health declined, that business, his life's work, was in limbo.

Because legacy isn't just built on hard work.

It's built on transferable value.

And Link knew it. He had started making the right moves.

Maintenance Contracts: He was learning how to create recurring revenue, a way to increase the value of his business while making things easier for customers.

Documentation Efforts: Even though he wasn't tech-savvy, he kept handwritten records of every customer, every system, every service call, proof that his business had tangible value beyond himself.

Mentorship: He trained younger techs, showing them his work ethic, his attention to detail, his way of treating customers.

But there wasn't enough time. Link's story ended before he could fully put the pieces together.

And that's why you don't wait to build your legacy.

You don't wait until you're tired.

You don't wait until you're forced to step away.

You don't wait until you have no choice.

DAVE: FROM MICROMANAGER TO LEADER

Then there's Dave.

For years, he ran his business like a dictatorship. He was the best at the technical work, and he made sure everyone knew it.

But when Brent, the future of his company, walked out the door, when Mike nearly quit, when his entire crew was one bad day away from leaving him behind, Dave finally woke up.

And he made a choice.

He stopped micromanaging and started trusting his team.

He built real systems so the business didn't depend entirely on him.

He learned from mentors like Tom and Frank, men who had already walked this path.

He created a leadership pipeline, making sure his team had a future beyond just working for Dave.

And what did that get him?

It got him a business that could actually outlast him.

It got him employees who WANTED to stay, who felt invested, who weren't looking for the next best offer.

It got him a life that wasn't consumed by stress, anxiety, and control.

Dave's story proves that culture is everything.

That leadership is learned, not just a title bestowed.

That your people are your biggest asset.

JACK: THE SPARK THAT CHANGED EVERYTHING

Jack had always been a great electrician. He ran a profitable business. But when a local private school asked about a service contract, something clicked.

He realized that his customers, his BEST customers, were calling him nine or ten times a year.

So why not create a predictable, reliable stream of income?

He started selling maintenance contracts, giving clients discounts on materials in exchange for a locked-in service agreement.

That stabilized his revenue, making it easier to forecast and grow.

Those contracts turned into bigger projects, like the $100,000 rewiring job for a manufacturing facility that never would have happened without that ongoing relationship.

Jack learned that repeat business isn't an accident.

It's strategic.

SARAH: THE MARKETING MACHINE

Sarah had the opposite problem.

She wasn't worried about recurring revenue; she had it.

She wasn't worried about customer service; her team was excellent.

What Sarah needed was a way to ensure her business stayed relevant, even when she wasn't actively selling.

She turned her website into a 24/7 lead-generating machine.

She implemented automation so potential customers stayed engaged.

She built a referral program that turned her best clients into brand ambassadors.

What's the lesson?

Being great at your work isn't enough.

People need to REMEMBER you.

You don't build a legacy by being the best-kept secret.

SO, WHAT'S YOUR LEGACY?

If you disappeared tomorrow, what would happen?

Would your business keep running?

Would your employees stay?

Would your clients even know where to turn?

Or would everything fall apart?

THE 5 KEY MOVES TO CREATE TRANSFERABLE VALUE

If you want your business to outlive you, you need to start NOW.

1. Document Everything.

- Create SOPs (Standard Operating Procedures) so someone else can do what you do.

- Invest in CRM and scheduling systems so customer data isn't just in your head.

2. Build a Leadership Pipeline.

- Start mentoring employees to take on bigger roles.
- Have a plan for who could replace you one day.

3. Create Recurring Revenue Streams.

- Sell maintenance contracts or subscription-based services.
- Find ways to get paid BEFORE the work happens.

4. Strengthen Your Company Culture.

- Employees stay where they feel valued.
- Make sure your leadership style isn't driving people away.

5. Plan Your Exit, NOW.

- Whether you sell, pass it down, or transition out, have a roadmap.
- Make sure your business is financially attractive to a future buyer.

FINAL THOUGHT: THE LEGACY LINK

The Legacy Link isn't a piece of paper.
It's not just your name on a building.
It's not just the work you've done.
It's the business you leave behind.

Link Helmandollar built a legacy of hard work, but not one that could continue without him.

Dave almost lost his company because he didn't see the bigger picture.

Jack figured out how to make his business work for him, not the other way around.

Sarah ensured that her business never stopped growing, even when she wasn't working.

So now, the question is about you.

- Are you building a job? Or are you building a business?
- Are you creating something that runs because of you, or something that will run without you?
- If you walked away today, would your business survive?

Because real legacy isn't just what you build.

It's what you leave behind.

Start building it today.

ACKNOWLEDGMENTS

Writing this book was more than just putting words on a page, it was a trek through my memories and a journey, one I could not have completed without the love, support, and unwavering belief of the people in my life.

To my Momma, Connie Helmandollar, my first and fiercest cheerleader. You have always believed in me, even when I didn't believe in myself. Your strength, your love, and your unshakable support have been my foundation. Thank you for reminding me who I am and for always being there.

To Kent, no dream has ever been too big, no idea too wild for you to stand beside me. Through every late night, every shift in direction, and every moment of self-doubt, you have been my constant. Your quiet support is the strength beneath my ambition, and I am endlessly grateful for you.

To my children, Wade, Vi, and Wyatt, you are the greatest joy of my life.

Wade, your accomplishments leave me in awe daily. To say I am proud is an understatement. But beyond your skills in the cockpit, you are a servant leader, a man respected and loved for your willingness to help anyone who needs your knowledge or expertise.

Vi, you are my right hand, my voice of reason, and a person who holds so much wisdom beyond your years. I could not do this without you. You have your grandmother's strength and your own brand of brilliance, and I am forever grateful for you.

Wyatt, my deep thinker, my conversationalist, my gourmet cohort, you see the world differently, and that is your gift. Whatever path you take, I know you will do great things. Maybe, just maybe, this book will be a stepping stone for you as you consider your future (in whatever industry steals your heart).

To Carina, when you became part of our family, you expanded the sum total of people we get to love. Your family has become our family, and ours has become yours. I call you my daughter-in-love because that's exactly what you are. What we share is uncommon, and I am so incredibly grateful for you. You are a force of love, intelligence, and dedication. Thank you for loving Wade, and I know you will be the most incredible mother to Madisen.

To Dylan, you are a force of nature, a whirlwind of brilliance and courage. Watching you build your own empire has been incredible, and I have no doubt that your vision will continue to grow and thrive. Thank you for loving my daughter so well.

To Mandy and Sydney, no words are adequate to capture my gratitude. While I was caring for my daddy, you carried our business on your shoulders. You gave me the gift of time with him, and that is something I can never repay. You held everything together, and because of you, I was able to be where I needed to be without worry. Thank you for your strength, your dedication, and for proving what I already knew: You are extraordinary.

To KJ, my dear friend of twenty years, my partner-in-mischief, my sounding board, my ride-or-die. You have been beside me through life's wild twists and turns, and there's no one else I'd rather conspire with.

To the rest of my team, Lacey, Leann, Nickie, your talent, support, and belief in our mission inspire me daily.

Lacey, you are a light in this world. You can find grace in a mud puddle, and that is a rare and beautiful gift.

Leann, you bring talent, organization, humor, and a shared literary nerdiness that I treasure.

Nickie, thank God for you, for your laughter, your zany personality, and your complete seriousness when it comes to getting the money.

Finally, to my clients, thank you for your trust, your friendship, and your willingness to let me into your businesses and dreams. You inspire me daily. It is because of you that I do what I do.

This book is not just mine; it belongs to all of you. Thank you, from the deepest part of my heart.

ABOUT THE AUTHOR

Tess Helmandollar grew up with an appreciation for hard work, legacy, and the power of building something that lasts. Inspired by her father's entrepreneurial journey, she developed a passion for helping business owners create transferable value, ensuring their companies can thrive beyond them.

As an entrepreneur, strategist, and visionary, Tess has spent years refining systems that empower businesses to scale, transition, and grow sustainably. As the owner of a thriving marketing agency and a HubSpot partner, she brings a wealth of experience in branding, automation, and business optimization, helping companies increase their impact and long-term value.

Beyond her work, Tess finds joy in the life she has built with her husband, Kent, as they embrace their empty nest, aside from two old, fat dogs. Her children have built lives of their own: Wade and his wife, Carina, are expecting their first child, Madisen Rosa, this summer, making Tess an excited soon-to-be Gigi. Vi, married to Dylan, works alongside Tess as the VP of Operations in their marketing agency. Wyatt, the youngest, rounds out the family's next generation of dreamers and doers.

A lifelong learner, Tess is fascinated by quantum physics, systems thinking, and the unseen forces that shape success. When she's not crafting business strategies, she enjoys traveling, writing, and embracing the moments that make life truly valuable.